The Art of Adulting: A Guidebook

Mastering the Art of Independence and
Personal Growth with Practical Tips
and Wise Advice

Plus
Calendars, Planners & Other Tools

THE ART OF ADULTING: A GUIDEBOOK
Mastering the Art of Independence and Personal Growth with Practical Tips and Wise Advice
Plus Calendars, Planners & Other Tools
All Rights Reserved
v1.0

ISBN: 9798320498072

Idea Tree Publishing

"Growing old is mandatory:
growing up is optional."

– Chili Davis

TABLE of CONTENTS

> "Youth is the gift of nature, but age is a work of art."
> - Stanislaw Jerzy Lec

FITNESS

CAR OWNERSHIP

RENTING, ROOMMATES & LANDLORDS

PERSONAL GROWTH

MORE

QUICK Reference GUIDE

How To Use This Book

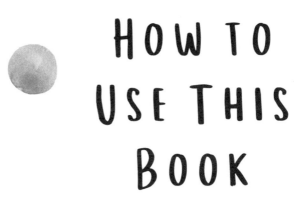

Read the book front to back or flip through the sections in whatever order you want, just make sure you check out all our adulting tips, tricks, and sage advice! Because hey, who says you have to learn adulting the hard way?

Use some or all of the templates, checklists, and schedules to create your own personalized routine to keep adult life running smoothly, so you can focus on the important stuff. For that, check out the last section. .

The book is made for you to write in, but feel free to make extra copies of the pages that are the most useful (for personal use only please).

As you read through it, use the Notes pages in the back to summarize the key points you want to focus on or remember.

This book scratches the surface of some very complicated and deep topics. Let it inspire you to dive deeper and learn more on your own. The world is vast, so explore it!

*"Life is 10% what happens to us and
90% how we react to it."*

— Charles R. Swindoll

AH YES, Adulthood

Ever feel like ice cream for breakfast?

Go for it, you're the boss! Want to sleep 'til noon or binge-watch cat videos with zero judgment? Your house, your rules! How about an inflatable hot tub in your living-room? Who would say no? (Unfortunately, as the adult you're the one who has to deal with the landlord about the foot of water in the hallway at 2am after SOMEONE drops a glass and a shard cuts a hole... but anyway).

Adulthood, finally! For the very first time all the dreams you've had actually seem within reach! At long last your passions will make you rich and the legacy you leave will change the world! Absolutely, yes! But first, we must plan.

Having the dream is one thing, getting there is another. Now that you're an adult, you can handle the hard reality - success takes all kinds of hard work - and if your laundry is piling up, your internet isn't paid, and you feel like you're in a hole you can't get out of, well, success is even harder. So first, we must organize.

Ever get excited about a paycheck only to see it vanish into a black hole of bills? Yep, welcome aboard the Adulting Express! First, we must budget.

Most adults get this far, but still end up feeling like success and fulfillment are always just around the corner. Only the wisest adults - the Legendary Adults - know that getting a handle on all the boring grown-up stuff is only important because it allows you to focus on what's really important: consciously creating that glorious life you've dreamed of and becoming the person who will make it all happen. More than that, it's learning to enjoy that crazy ride. Everything you've dreamed of is really possible, but it won't fall out of the sky. You have to do your part. So go ahead and get out there - the world is your oyster. With everything in this guidebook, you'll be a legendary adult in no time!

Just don't forget about that laundry piling up and to grab milk on the way home. And just a reminder to finally make that dentist appointment, and you're out of bandaids too. Oh, and don't forget to send a card to grandma for her birthday next month, plus it's your boss's son's graduation next week... wait, did you pay that phone bill last month??

Just use the book.

Happy Adulting!

SO...
YOU LIVE ON YOUR OWN NOW!
THAT MEANS YOU NEED STUFF. BORING ADULT STUFF LIKE BANDAIDS AND LIGHTBULBS AND...YOU KNOW, STUFF

Unfortunately, adulting means a lot more trips to boring stores to give them money for things you never had to pay for before. One of the many prices of being an adult. At least you can save some time by using this reference list to make sure you have everything you need in your new home, and always have the basic necessities on hand.

- String
- Tape

(Regular, duct, and electrical)

- Elastic Bands
- Scissors
- Paper & Pens
- Permanent Marker
- Push Pins
- Screwdriver Set
- Hammer
- Picture Nails & Anchors
- Lightbulbs
- Flashlight
- Extra Batteries
- Lighter or Matches
- Fire Extinguisher (ABC type)
- Carbon Monoxide Monitor

- Umbrella
- Doormat
- Watering Can
- Laundry Basket
- Curtains & Curtain Rods
- Bedsheets & Comforter
- Extra Blanket
- Bed Pillows
- Dish Drying Rack
- Dish Towels
- Dishes & Cutlery

(at least 4 of everything, glasses, mugs, big plates AND small plates, forks, knives, spoons)

- Garbage bins

(larger one for the kitchen, smaller ones for the bathrooms)

APPLIANCES
- Toaster
- Microwave
- Blender
- Coffee Maker
- Kettle

  - KITCHEN TOOLS

  (see cooking section)

  - CLEANING SUPPLIES

  (see cleaning section)

OTHER STUFF YOU MAY NEED TO BUY
ON A REGULAR BASIS:

- Plastic Wrap
- Aluminum Foil
- Sandwich Bags
- Garbage/ Recycling Bags
- Paper Towel
- Dish Soap
- Laundry Detergent

PRO TIP
If it's not too heavy, the next time you want to hang a small picture or something on your wall, try a push pin instead of a nail. Super easy, and no hammer involved!

Bathroom Stuff

- Shower Curtain
- Floor Mat
- Soapdish
- Loofah
- Shower Caddy
- Towels
- Handtowels (for guests!)
- Hairbrush or Comb

More Stuff To Pick Up Regularly:

- Deoderant
- Body Lotion
- Body Wash
- Toilet Paper
- Soap
- Shampoo & Conditioner
- Toothbrush & Toothpaste

Medicine Cabinet

There are a few things that any doctor will tell you to keep on hand at home in case of illness or emergency.

- Acetaminophen and/or Ibuprofen Tablets (for pain or fever)
- Antacid (for upset stomach)
- Antibiotic Cream or Gel (for cuts, scrapes or burns)
- Hydrogen Peroxide (for cleaning wounds)
- Antihistamine (liquid, for fast absorption)
- Bandaids of Various Sizes
- Thermometer
- Gel Ice Pack (keep it in the freezer)
- Heating Pad or Heat Pack (to heat in the microwave)

HOW TO HANG STUFF UP
(The Proper Way)

Find the Stud

The surface half inch of a wall is usually drywall, which is very crumbly and causes any nail or screw to loosen easily over time. Nails or screws are much sturdier when secured into wood. Studs are the wooden beams which make up the frame of the wall. Although you can't see them, hanging things on studs will be much sturdier.

Find the stud either with a stud finder device, or by knocking on the wall. Start from the edge and knock along the wall moving inward. Listen for changes in the sound. A hollow sound typically indicates that you're tapping on the space between studs, while a solid, dull thud suggests that you've hit a stud.

Use an Anchor

If you can't find the stud or it's not where you want the picture to be, use a wall anchor. These are plastic holders that go into the drywall and then expand when a screw is inserted into it, creating a secure hold.

First, select the right anchor based on the weight of the picture and size of the screw or nail. Drill a hole in the wall and tap the wall anchor into the hole with a hammer until its flush with the wall surface. Finally, screw or hammer the hardware into the anchor, and hang your picture securely on the wall.

The screw or nail goes in here —

Wall anchors come in different sizes. Make sure you get the right size for your nail and weight of the thing you're hanging. You should also consider the depth of the wall which you're hammering into. Drywall is usually between 1/2 and 5/8 of an inch.

These wooden beams where the wall will be are called STUDS. You can see them here before the insulation and drywall has been installed to complete the wall.

FLOOR PLAN IDEAS FOR A SQUARE LIVING ROOM

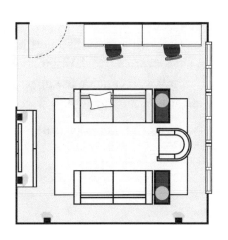

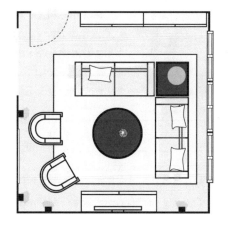

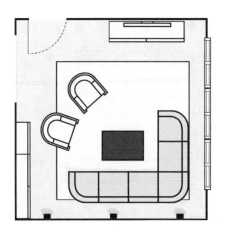

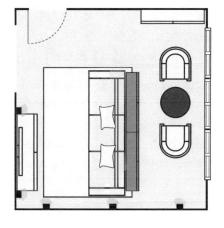

KEEPING SAFE AT HOME
4 Steps

1. FIRE

It's important to keep a fire extinguisher in or near your kitchen. When you use a fire extinguisher, point the spray towards the base of the fire.

- Fire needs 3 things- heat, oxygen, and fuel. Take any one of these away and the fire goes out.
- Never attach multiple extension cords together - it's an electrical fire waiting to happen!
- Grease fires cannot be put out with water! If something on the stove catches fire, aside from a fire extinguisher (which includes the 'B' symbol), you can use baking soda or cover it with a lid (to eliminate the oxygen).

EXTINGUISHERS ARE CLASSIFIED BY WHICH TYPE OF BURNING MATERIAL IT CAN EXTINGUISH (CLASS A, B, OR C). GET ONE THAT IS LABELED ABC SO IT CAN PUT OUT ANY TYPE OF COMMON HOUSE FIRE.

COMMON TYPES OF FIRES:

CLASS A: Combustible Material (wood, fabric, etc)
CLASS B: Grease & Oil (cooking oil, engine grease, etc)
CLASS C: Electrical (Faulty appliances, overloaded circuits, etc)

2. CARBON MONOXIDE

Carbon monoxide (CO) is a colourless, odourless gas that is produced by the incomplete combustion of fuels like gas and oil which are used to cook and heat most homes. It's extra scary because you can't smell or taste it even when you're breathing it in! Exposure can be fatal.

CO MONITORS ARE CHEAP AND CAN SAVE YOUR LIFE.
THEY PLUG IN THE WALL AND YOU NEED TO REPLACE THEM EVERY 5 YEARS.
SOME SMOKE DETECTORS HAVE BUILT-IN CO MONITORS, BUT NOT ALL.

3. CHEMICALS

There are positives and negatives about having chemicals in your home. They can make cleaning easier, but there are a few risks to keep in mind:

- **Fire Hazards**, if the chemical is flammable
- **Combustibles**, aerosol cans and compressed gases, don't leave them close to a heat source
- **Toxicity**, don't let your dog lick it up!
- **Corrosion**, these chemicals destroy your skin on contact
- **Allergic Reaction**, if you have unexplained rashes, itchiness or puffiness, it may be because of a chemical you just used

IF USING HARSH CHEMICALS LIKE PAINT THINNER, BLEACH, OR OVEN CLEANER ALWAYS OPEN THE WINDOW FOR VENTILATION. WORK OUTSIDE IF YOU CAN. ALWAYS USE GLOVES AND EYE PROTECTION.

NEVER MIX!!!

Mixing certain cleaning ingredients can produce toxic fumes like chlorine gas. These can make you sick and even cause organ damage.

BLEACH & VINEGAR

Never Mix Bleach with:

- ✖ Glass Cleaner (Ammonia)
- ✖ Hydrogen Peroxide
- ✖ Rubbing Alcohol

Vinegar & Hydrogen Peroxide, a dangerous mix!

4. BREAK-INS & WEIRDOS

- Lock your doors and windows!!
- Don't give your address out online.
- If you're iffy about a stranger you're talking to at your door, casually mention your (perhaps non-existent) roommate/ partner/ large intimidating person who's "inside".
- Close the curtains and leave a light on if you're away overnight.
- Leave a spare key with a neighbour you trust, not under the mat.

Practice awareness. It's not about being paranoid, just smart and observant. Are the doors locked? Is the stove off? Should you call your landlord about that outlet that sparks sometimes? Yes! Yes you should!

The average employee spends nearly an hour of their workday on their phone.

Studies show that natural light improves productivity.

Globally, people average 6 hours and 58 minutes of screen time per day. Daily screen time has increased by nearly 50 minutes per day since 2013.

On average, people spend 1-2 hours per day on chores like cooking, cleaning, and laundry.

TIME MANAGEMENT

Time is Your Most Valuable Adulting Asset

Adulting involves a lot of juggling. You have to make money, you have a social life, maybe you're in school, plus you have to buy groceries and pay the water bill, probably deal with a clogged drain... and that's on a good day.

Rookie adult mistakes like not organizing your time can cost you a lot. What you do with your time is going to either launch you towards success or keep you dragging your feet in the mud of chaos. Life passes by faster and faster as you get older, so start thinking of your time as valuable. Spend some time up front planning, so you can make best use of the rest of it.

Feeling Overwhelmed?

Simply writing things down makes all the tasks you have to do seem a lot more manageable. Once you do this it's all right in front of you, you know you won't forget anything, and now you can prioritize. A piece of advice: pick the hardest most daunting task to do first. It's all downhill from there. After that it's easy!

Whenever you feel overwhelmed with the sheer amount of things on your agenda, pretend thet first thing on your list is the only one you have to do, and just get it done. Then, oh look, there's another thing... so get that one done next. And so on. No stress. One thing at a time. Scheduling is about not wasting time, so you can spend more time doing things that you enjoy and enrich you. Moreover, it allows you the freedom to look ahead and consciously plan the life you want to build for yourself.

Pro Tip: Time Blocking

Time blocking involves assigning specific time blocks for different activities throughout the day. Assign daily time blocks for tasks like checking email, working on projects, and personal activities. By dedicating uninterrupted time to specific tasks, you can increase productivity, reduce procrastination, and maintain better balance in your life.

SCHEDULES & TO-DO LISTS

However you want to schedule things for yourself, you do you. Personally I am partial to the sticky note - great for a quick to-do list. The important thing is, you remember stuff!

PHONE

Your phone or tablet likely comes with planner and calendar apps you can use. Or, find a scheduling app that's better suited to your needs.

Pro Tip:
Reminder Apps (with alarms!)

If you are a brave enough adult to admit that having cat memes at your fingertips while trying to schedule your life can be distracting (kudos to you), then try a real live paper agenda. Or, if you prefer a less structured approach, maybe To-Do lists are right for you. The next few pages have some examples you can write on, make copies of, or use for inspiration.

DAILY

Daily agendas are highly recommended for those who have a lot to do and who know that if it's not written down it's not getting done - not to mention the sheer joy of crossing off all those tasks once they're done!

WEEKLY

Weekly agendas have one week per page, or sometimes a few days per page. These are great for those who use other tools as well, like to do lists, for some of their other adulting duties.

MONTHLY

Monthly agendas are basically calendars to go. They help keep you on top of the bigger things like appointments, events, and important deadlines.

DAILY PLANNER

DATE

M	T	W	T	F	S	S

6:00	
7:00	
8:00	
9:00	
10:00	
11:00	
12:00	
13:00	
14:00	
15:00	
16:00	
17:00	
18:00	
19:00	
20:00	
21:00	
22:00	
23:00	

TOP 3 PRIORITIES

-
-
-

REMINDERS

FOR TOMORROW

Notes

Daily Planner

DATE

| M | T | W | T | F | S | S |

6:00

7:00

8:00

9:00

10:00

11:00

12:00

13:00

14:00

15:00

16:00

17:00

18:00

19:00

20:00

21:00

22:00

23:00

TOP 3 PRIORITIES

-
-
-

REMINDERS

FOR TOMORROW

Notes

DAILY PLANNER

Schedule

Time	
6:00	
7:00	
8:00	
9:00	
10:00	
11:00	
12:00	
1:00	
2:00	
3:00	
4:00	
5:00	
6:00	
7:00	
8:00	
9:00	

Top priorities

- [ ]
- [ ]
- [ ]
- [ ]
- [ ]
- [ ]
- [ ]
- [ ]
- [ ]
- [ ]
- [ ]
- [ ]
- [ ]
- [ ]
- [ ]

Notes

DAILY PLANNER

Schedule

6:00	
7:00	
8:00	
9:00	
10:00	
11:00	
12:00	
1:00	
2:00	
3:00	
4:00	
5:00	
6:00	
7:00	
8:00	
9:00	

Top priorities

- ☐
- ☐
- ☐
- ☐
- ☐
- ☐
- ☐
- ☐
- ☐
- ☐
- ☐
- ☐
- ☐
- ☐
- ☐
- ☐

Notes

Weekly Planner

PRIORITIES

- _____
- _____
- _____
- _____
- _____

MONDAY   Date: _____

- _____
- _____
- _____
- _____

TUESDAY   Date: _____

- _____
- _____
- _____
- _____

REMINDERS

WEDNESDAY   Date: _____

- _____
- _____
- _____
- _____

THURSDAY   Date: _____

- _____
- _____
- _____
- _____

NEXT WEEK

FRIDAY   Date: _____

- _____
- _____
- _____
- _____

Notes

SATURDAY   Date: _____

- _____
- _____
- _____
- _____

SUNDAY   Date: _____

- _____
- _____
- _____
- _____

Weekly Planner

PRIORITIES

○ _____
○ _____
○ _____
○ _____
○ _____

MONDAY   Date: _____
○ _____
○ _____
○ _____
○ _____

TUESDAY   Date: _____
○ _____
○ _____
○ _____
○ _____

REMINDERS

WEDNESDAY   Date: _____
○ _____
○ _____
○ _____
○ _____

THURSDAY   Date: _____
○ _____
○ _____
○ _____
○ _____

NEXT WEEK

FRIDAY   Date: _____
○ _____
○ _____
○ _____
○ _____

Notes

SATURDAY   Date: _____
○ _____
○ _____
○ _____
○ _____

SUNDAY   Date: _____
○ _____
○ _____
○ _____
○ _____

CALENDAR

Monthly

JAN	FEB	MAR	APR	MAY	JUN
JUL	AUG	SEP	OCT	NOV	DEC

Sunday	Monday	Tuesday	Wednesday	Thursday	Friday	Saturday

Notes

CALENDAR

Monthly

JAN	FEB	MAR	APR	MAY	JUN
JUL	AUG	SEP	OCT	NOV	DEC

Sunday	Monday	Tuesday	Wednesday	Thursday	Friday	Saturday

Notes

TO-DO LIST

DATE: / /

● ● ● ● ● ● ●
S M T W T F S

- ☐ ....
- ☐ ....
- ☐ ....
- ☐ ....
- ☐ ....
- ☐ ....
- ☐ ....
- ☐ ....
- ☐ ....
- ☐ ....
- ☐ ....
- ☐ ....
- ☐ ....
- ☐ ....
- ☐ ....
- ☐ ....
- ☐ ....
- ☐ ....
- ☐ ....
- ☐ ....
- ☐ ....
- ☐ ....
- ☐ ....
- ☐ ....

Notes

TO-DO LIST

DATE: / /

● ● ● ● ● ● ●
S M T W T F S

- ☐ ....
- ☐ ....
- ☐ ....
- ☐ ....
- ☐ ....
- ☐ ....
- ☐ ....
- ☐ ....
- ☐ ....
- ☐ ....
- ☐ ....
- ☐ ....
- ☐ ....
- ☐ ....
- ☐ ....
- ☐ ....
- ☐ ....
- ☐ ....
- ☐ ....
- ☐ ....
- ☐ ....
- ☐ ....
- ☐ ....

Notes

WEEKLY TO-DO LIST

WEEK OF: _ _ _ _ _ _ _

MONDAY

1
2
3
4
5
6
7
8
9

TUESDAY

1
2
3
4
5
6
7
8
9

WEDNESDAY

1
2
3
4
5
6
7
8
9

THURSDAY

1
2
3
4
5
6
7
8
9

FRIDAY

1
2
3
4
5
6
7
8
9

SATURDAY

1
2
3
4
5
6
7
8
9

SUNDAY

1
2
3
4
5
6
7
8
9

NOTES

WEEKLY TO-DO LIST

WEEK OF: ------------------------

MONDAY
1
2
3
4
5
6
7
8
9

TUESDAY
1
2
3
4
5
6
7
8
9

WEDNESDAY
1
2
3
4
5
6
7
8
9

THURSDAY
1
2
3
4
5
6
7
8
9

FRIDAY
1
2
3
4
5
6
7
8
9

SATURDAY
1
2
3
4
5
6
7
8
9

SUNDAY
1
2
3
4
5
6
7
8
9

NOTES

BIRTHDAY CALENDAR

*Because an adult never forgets a birthday**

JANUARY	FEBRUARY	MARCH

APRIL	MAY	JUNE

JULY	AUGUST	SEPTEMBER

OCTOBER	NOVEMBER	DECEMBER

*or at least tries very hard not to

Did You Know:

The tradition of putting candles on a birthday cake dates back to ancient Greece when people would offer moon-shaped cakes to Artemis, the goddess of the moon, to honour her. The lit candles on the cake symbolized the glow of the moon.

Help Maiko navigate
THE WORST TRAFFIC CIRCLE IN THE WORLD
to get to her important job on time!

Did You Know...

In London, Cologne, and Amsterdam, drivers spend more than 50 hours a year in road traffic congestion! This number increases to 70 hours for drivers in Paris and Manchester.

GETTING A JOB
(AND KEEPING IT)

This isn't your after school job at the bowling alley here. It's time to put on your grown-up pants now, the roof over your head depends on it. That's okay, it's just the typical adulting stuff. Of course you want to do well, and we have some great advice coming up about first getting the job and then, naturally, crushing it.

Your first few jobs will teach you a lot about what you do and don't want in your future. See it as a continuation of your education, only this time you get paid for it!

RESUMÉS *Make Yours Stand Out*

Chances are you already have a resumé, or at least you know there are a million templates and formulas you can find online. But here are some Pro Tips to help yours make it to the interview pile.

- **Make It Look Good**, and for goodness sake, use proper formatting! No one is impressed by a resume that is disorganized, hard to read, and all in the same sized font.
- **Upload Your Own Resumé** if you're applying using an online platform. This makes you look more professional, having taken that extra step to make the best impression possible, instead of using the generic fill-in-the-blank template the platform gives you.
- **Include Key Words From the Job Posting** in your resumé and cover letter. If thats what they're looking for, show them thats exactly what you have.
- **Include Any Leadership Experience**, no matter how small or seemingly insignificant. Mangers are looking for people who have confidence in themselves and are able to put themselves out there and successfully take the initiative to handle situations and role model that for others.
- **Include a Cover Letter.** These are gold. Again - make SURE it's been edited and double-checked because nothing makes a worse impression than bad grammar or spelling errors.

Contract Work: As a contractor, you technically work for yourself, providing your services. You pay your own taxes and the company doesn't pay into Employment Insurance or Pension. However this model allows some greater flexibility for the contractor.

Salary: This type of pay comes with a guaranteed amount of money annually. Usually you work full-time (35-40 hrs per week) and receive benefits like medical insurance, as well as paid vacation and sick time which may increase over the years. Statutory holidays are paid too.

INTERVIEWS *Crush it With These Pro Tips*

An interview is your time to shine! Convince yourself you are perfect for this job, even if it's out of your comfort zone. You're going for a balance of confidence and humility - you have everything it takes to succeed in the role, including a willingness to learn and grow. Managers love seeing passion for the work, and will give a job to someone who seems excited to learn over someone who has tons of experience but lacks initiative.

- Be on time!
- Research the company and role ahead of time.
- Fake it 'til you make it - act the part even if you feel out of place.
- Look them in the eyes (with breaks - let's not be creepy!)
- Look neat and wear professional clothes
   (no sweatpants, jeans, or workout clothes).
- Take off your coat during the interview.
- Put your phone on silent and put it away!
- Bring references and any relevant documents with you.
- Show them you are interested in learning and growth.
- When they give you a chance to ask questions, make sure you have a couple prepared.

Common Interview Questions
...to think about ahead of time

- **What interests you in this role / this field?**

Ideally you really would have interest in the job. Enjoying your work will definitely help you to be successful. If not, consider if this job is really the right path for you. And maybe it is for now, just not long-term. Just don't mention that at the interview!

- **Why are you the best candidate for this job?**

This doesn't have to have to do with the most experience. Skills can be taught. Passion, dedication, and initiative is either there or it isn't, and those are the keys to success in any role.

- **How does your experience lend itself to this position?**

Even if you have no experience, talk about anything related to the role, even in your personal life. Then describe your interest in learning more and how your broader skills - communication, writing, problem-solving, etc - will be useful to the company.

- **Describe a time you made a mistake and how you handled it.**

Someone claiming never to have messed up is a huge red flag. It's ok to admit to mistakes! Managers ask this because they want to see that you can learn and grow from your mistakes (and not make them a second time).

- **What are your greatest strengths / weaknesses?**

Greatest strengths are easy. As for weaknesses, think of ones that can indicate positive qualities as well, like a tendency to take on too many tasks at once. Then MAKE SURE you go on to explain strategies you've ALREADY developed to counter these things and turn them into positives. Everyone has flaws, but the most valuable employees know what theirs are and work on them on a regular basis.

How To BE A GOOD EMPLOYEE

For managers, there's nothing better than a good employee who does the job, can be trusted, and works well with the rest of the team - no drama.

Actually, you only need two arms for this...

It's that simple. Managers spend much of their time dealing with consequences of drama instead of actually participating in the functioning of the company, which is what they actually want to do. Make their lives easier in this way and TRUST ME, they will go out of their way to help you right back (the good ones anyway). This will make your job a heck of a lot more pleasant! Plus, doing the job well and being a good team member are obviously important on their own accord. You'll actually learn things, be more likely to receive a promotion, and will be given more growth opportunities. Plus it's a lot more satisfying and actually easier to be committed to doing a good job, rather than always trying to figure out how to get out of things.

Take any and all opportunities to learn new skills and grow. Those who do are the people who get promoted later on.

When bringing issues to your boss, come up with some possible solutions first to present along with the problem.

Be reliable and honest. Don't cover things up for yourself or others, and admit to your mistakes before they cause bigger problems.

Ask questions if you need to! Statistics say new employees only feel comfortable asking questions for three months, but actually take about 6 months to a year to fully adapt to a role. See the problem?

If you have an issue with a coworker, don't gossip about it. Tension in the workplace is a killer. Bring your issue to the person directly, respectfully. If that doesn't work, then ask for your manager's help.

Longterm GOALS

Ask any successful adult, and they'll tell you that goals are critical. It's not about meeting every goal you make; many of them you'll end up adjusting along the way, but if you don't have some end-point in mind, you'll end up going wherever the tide takes you. That may not always be bad, but it's hard being 40 and realizing there's still a whole life you want that you haven't started yet!

Spend some time thinking about the future and jot down a few points on the next couple pages. Where do you want to be in 5 years, 10 years, 15 years? What kind of life do you want to have?

Figuring out where you want to get to is step one.

The next step is planning all those little steps you need to take to get from here to there. If you're unsure, try thinking backwards. What would be the very last step before you reached the goal? What about the second last? Keep going. Remember, breaking anything down into more manageable steps makes any complex task seem way more achievable. Then you need to act on it! If you're still unsure, do anything you can think of to get yourself going in the right direction. Baby steps are still steps, and it's always worth asking other adults questions about how they got to where they are, if that's somewhere you think you want to get to as well. Think about your future regularly. Be real with yourself about the circumstances you're dealing with so you can plan accordingly and set yourself up for the very best success.

VISION BOARDS

Our minds are more powerful than we know. Many believe that focusing your conscious thoughts onto an idea can help manifest it into reality. At the very least, doing this would help to keep your goals front of mind.

A vision board is a place you can put images, words, whatever represents for you your vision for your future. Hang it up somewhere that you'll see it every day.

Some say the act of 'wishing' or 'wanting' something will simply bring you more of the wishing and wanting. Instead, adopt a mentality of acceptance. This WILL come to pass. Everyday, visualize it. Use your senses to imagine what it will be like, what you'll feel like, what it will smell and sound like. A vision board can help. Getting used to feeling like the person who lives that life will help you overcome mental barriers, like that deep-rooted fear that many of us have of not being good enough to achieve what we want. We are! But we have to believe it, first.

good things take time

GOALS
FOR THE YEAR

DATE SET: _____.

WORK / CAREER / MONEY

FUN / LEISURE

PERSONAL GROWTH

HEALTH

HABITS

RELATIONSHIPS

"Success is stumbling from failure to failure with no loss of enthusiasm."
-WINSTON S CHURCHILL

5 YEARS

_____
_____
_____
_____
_____
_____
_____

10 YEARS

_____
_____
_____
_____
_____
_____
_____
_____

15 YEARS

_____
_____
_____
_____
_____
_____
_____
_____

MONEY
HOW TO TURN MONEY INTO *Wealth*

Were you ever told to just find a job you love to do and you'll never work a day in your life?

Well, it's grown-up time now, and unfortunately there is a lot more to it than that. In today's world, rising inflation (stuff getting more expensive), high interest rates, and crazy competition in many markets, plus wages not keeping pace, it's harder than ever to get ahead. (Unless you have a guidebook on adulting of course). It's nice to think money isn't that important, and in itself it's not, but in today's society money is a necessary tool that everyone needs in order to find any degree of self-determination and freedom, and that's TRUE wealth.

When it comes to money make sure you set short and long-term goals, develop a good budget, and stick to it. Don't feel scared to look in your bank account. If you don't like what you see in there, or if you wish there was more, use the tools and follow the advice laid out here. Get excited about money! With a bit of discipline in your early adulting career, trust me, you'll put yourself miles ahead of the pack on the way to your best life. Money can't buy happiness, but it can allow for so many more opportunities and possibilities. It will allow you freedom to make choices in your life that you wouldn't otherwise have.

THE SIDE-GIG ECONOMY

Many people young and old are looking for extra ways of earning money. Maybe with a job you make ends meet, but you can do better than that. Side-gigs are often things you enjoy and are good at, that you simply figure out a way to monetize. Some examples might be a part-time job, selling a service, self-publishing, or online copywriting. Get out of your comfort zone and you'll be surprised how far you can go.

PASSIVE INCOME

This means sources of income for which you do NO (or minimal) work to maintain. WHAT?! You say; THIS EXISTS?? Oh yes, it very much does! Owning rental properties, dividends, and royalties from books or downloadable products are common examples of passive income sources. Basically you do the work or pay a cost up front one time, and then sit back and reap the rewards.

Pro Tip

Have multiple income sources. Aside from your regular job, throw in a side gig that you actually like to do, plus a few passive income sources. When sh*t hits the fan, you'll be laughing! In fact, people leave their 9-5 jobs all time because their side-gigs start earning more money!

Automate Your Savings

Set up automatic transfers from your chequing account to your savings account each month. This ensures that you're consistently saving money without having to think about it.

Automate ALL your bills...

This will save you headaches and help keep your credit score high.

Pro Tip

Debt is a tricky thing. While you never want to get stuck in debt, it's good to run up a little debt which is quickly paid off. This is another way to build credit.

MONTHLY BUDGET

#1 Adulting Tool

INCOME

Source	Amount
	$
	$
	$
TOTAL	$

Make sure ALL sources of income are listed here.

MONTHLY EXPENSES

Description	Amount
	$
	$
	$
	$
	$
	$
	$
	$
	$
	$
	$
	$
	$
	$
TOTAL	$

Pro Tip:
Make a Savings Goal for the Year

Always budget savings into your expenses. Any part of your budget that's not spent will be extra savings.

Bills (like internet, hydro, rent) should each have their own line. This kind of expense doesn't usually change month to month.

Group smaller expenses like shampoo or an event ticket into categories like household, personal care, vehicle expenses, etc.

What if your expenses are higher than your income?

Even if your income is juuuust enough to cover your expenses, you need to make some changes. Living paycheck to paycheck is simply not sustainable. Even if you're going to school and have a plan to make more in the future, you need savings for when an unexpected cost arises - which it always does.

- See if you can reduce expenses. Start tracking everything. You'll be surprised how much gets spent needlessly when you look back on it.
- Call your providers to negotiate lower fees
- Look for other sources of income

MONTHLY BUDGET

#1 Adulting Tool

INCOME

Source	Amount
	$
	$
	$
	$
	$
	$
TOTAL	$

Notes

MONTHLY EXPENSES

Description	Amount
	$
	$
	$
	$
	$
	$
	$
	$
	$
	$
	$
	$
	$
TOTAL	$

BUDGET TRACKER

JAN FEB MAR APR MAY JUN JUL AUG SEPT OCT NOV DEC

INCOME

Date	Source	Amount
		$
		$
		$
	TOTAL	$

FIXED EXPENSES

Date	Description	Amount
	Rent	$
	Utilities	$
	Phone	$
	Internet	$
	Savings Contribution	$
		$
		$
		$
		$
		$
		$
	TOTAL	$

OTHER EXPENSES

Description	Amount
Groceries	$
Household Supplies	$
Toiletries	$
Gas	$
Car Expense	$
Medical	$
Leisure Activities	$
Restaurants/Dine-In	$
	$
	$
	$
	$
TOTAL	$

How well did I Adult?

Total Income		Total Expense		Extra Savings
$	−	$	=	$

Budgeted Amount (preset)		Total Expense		Difference
$	−	$	=	$

If the Difference or Extra Savings is in the negative, review your expenses and see what you can change next month

Budget Tracker

JAN FEB MAR APR MAY JUN JUL AUG SEPT OCT NOV DEC

Income

Date	Source	Amount
		$
		$
		$
TOTAL		$

Fixed Expenses

Date	Description	Amount
	Rent	$
	Utilities	$
	Phone	$
	Internet	$
	Savings Contribution	$
		$
		$
		$
		$
		$
	TOTAL	$

Other Expenses

Description	Amount
Groceries	$
Household Supplies	$
Toiletries	$
Gas	$
Car Expense	$
Medical	$
Leisure Activities	$
Restaurants/Dine-In	$
	$
	$
	$
TOTAL	$

How well did I Adult?

Total Income		Total Expense		Extra Savings
$	−	$	=	$

Budgeted Amount (preset)		Total Expense		Difference
$	−	$	=	$

If the Difference or Extra Savings is in the negative, review your expenses and see what you can change next month

SERVICE & SUBSCRIPTION TRACKER
ALL YOUR PAID ACCOUNTS IN *One Place!*

Service / Subscription Name: _____

Account Details	Login Info	Recurring Cost	Frequency
Start Date:	Website:	$	☐ Weekly ☐ Monthly ☐ Yearly
Account #:	Username:		
Other:	Password:	☐ Auto-Renew ☐ Renew Date: _____

Service / Subscription Name: _____

Account Details	Login Info	Recurring Cost	Frequency
Start Date:	Website:	$	☐ Weekly ☐ Monthly ☐ Yearly
Account #:	Username:		
Other:	Password:	☐ Auto-Renew ☐ Renew Date: _____

Service / Subscription Name: _____

Account Details	Login Info	Recurring Cost	Frequency
Start Date:	Website:	$	☐ Weekly ☐ Monthly ☐ Yearly
Account #:	Username:		
Other:	Password:	☐ Auto-Renew ☐ Renew Date: _____

Service / Subscription Name: _____

Account Details	Login Info	Recurring Cost	Frequency
Start Date:	Website:	$	☐ Weekly ☐ Monthly ☐ Yearly
Account #:	Username:		
Other:	Password:	☐ Auto-Renew ☐ Renew Date: _____

SERVICE & SUBSCRIPTION TRACKER
ALL YOUR PAID ACCOUNTS IN *One Place!*

Service / Subscription Name: _____

Account Details	Login Info	Recurring Cost	Frequency
Start Date:	Website:	$	☐ Weekly
Account #:			☐ Monthly
	Username:		☐ Yearly
Other:	Password:	☐ Auto-Renew ☐ Renew Date: _____	

Service / Subscription Name: _____

Account Details	Login Info	Recurring Cost	Frequency
Start Date:	Website:	$	☐ Weekly
Account #:			☐ Monthly
	Username:		☐ Yearly
Other:	Password:	☐ Auto-Renew ☐ Renew Date: _____	

Service / Subscription Name: _____

Account Details	Login Info	Recurring Cost	Frequency
Start Date:	Website:	$	☐ Weekly
Account #:			☐ Monthly
	Username:		☐ Yearly
Other:	Password:	☐ Auto-Renew ☐ Renew Date: _____	

Service / Subscription Name: _____

Account Details	Login Info	Recurring Cost	Frequency
Start Date:	Website:	$	☐ Weekly
Account #:			☐ Monthly
	Username:		☐ Yearly
Other:	Password:	☐ Auto-Renew ☐ Renew Date: _____	

SERVICE & SUBSCRIPTION TRACKER
ALL YOUR PAID ACCOUNTS IN *One Place!*

Service / Subscription Name: _____

Account Details	Login Info	Recurring Cost	Frequency
Start Date:	Website:	$	☐ Weekly
Account #:			☐ Monthly
	Username:		☐ Yearly
Other:	Password:	☐ Auto-Renew	
		☐ Renew Date: _____	

Service / Subscription Name: _____

Account Details	Login Info	Recurring Cost	Frequency
Start Date:	Website:	$	☐ Weekly
Account #:			☐ Monthly
	Username:		☐ Yearly
Other:	Password:	☐ Auto-Renew	
		☐ Renew Date: _____	

Service / Subscription Name: _____

Account Details	Login Info	Recurring Cost	Frequency
Start Date:	Website:	$	☐ Weekly
Account #:			☐ Monthly
	Username:		☐ Yearly
Other:	Password:	☐ Auto-Renew	
		☐ Renew Date: _____	

Service / Subscription Name: _____

Account Details	Login Info	Recurring Cost	Frequency
Start Date:	Website:	$	☐ Weekly
Account #:			☐ Monthly
	Username:		☐ Yearly
Other:	Password:	☐ Auto-Renew	
		☐ Renew Date: _____	

SERVICE & SUBSCRIPTION TRACKER
ALL YOUR PAID ACCOUNTS IN *One Place!*

Service / Subscription Name: _____

Account Details	Login Info	Recurring Cost	Frequency
Start Date:	Website:	$	☐ weekly
Account #:			☐ Monthly
	username:		☐ yearly
Other:	Password:	☐ Auto-Renew	
		☐ Renew Date: _____	

Service / Subscription Name: _____

Account Details	Login Info	Recurring Cost	Frequency
Start Date:	Website:	$	☐ weekly
Account #:			☐ Monthly
	username:		☐ yearly
Other:	Password:	☐ Auto-Renew	
		☐ Renew Date: _____	

Service / Subscription Name: _____

Account Details	Login Info	Recurring Cost	Frequency
Start Date:	Website:	$	☐ weekly
Account #:			☐ Monthly
	username:		☐ yearly
Other:	Password:	☐ Auto-Renew	
		☐ Renew Date: _____	

Service / Subscription Name: _____

Account Details	Login Info	Recurring Cost	Frequency
Start Date:	Website:	$	☐ weekly
Account #:			☐ Monthly
	username:		☐ yearly
Other:	Password:	☐ Auto-Renew	
		☐ Renew Date: _____	

SAVINGS

Or, How to Reduce Your Adult Stress by 90%

Saving money doesn't mean putting cash under your mattress anymore. It means having a financial plan for when your car breaks down and your dog gets sick and you lose your job all in the same week. More importantly, it's also about starting to build your future. When you're 20 years old this concept seems so abstract, but ignoring it now will be devastating to you down the road. Spending everything you make because you know you can just make more is simply eating away at your future. It is literally the difference between being 45 years old in a rental unit wishing you could finally afford a nice vacation, and having no trouble packing your bags in the master bedroom of your own house and jetting off to a tropical beach. Now that you're an adult, you CAN'T ignore this part, so pay attention! This is your life we're talking about! The small savings decisions you make TODAY will have a big effect on you 10, 20, 30 years from now and beyond. I guarantee it.

Let me tell you another fact... **You will NEVER get rich on salary alone,** no matter what your job is. Saving comes first, but after that, investing is a MUST. The rich are rich because of compounding interest and asset growth - period.

> SAVING IS ALL ABOUT USING YOUR MONEY AS A TOOL TO PLAN AND CREATE THE FUTURE LIFE YOU WANT.

Even if you don't have specific financial goals in mind, saving money will allow you two huge freedoms:

1. **Freedom to rest easy even when a major expense suddenly pops up.**
2. **Freedom to know that when you are ready to make those big dreams a reality, you'll be able to do it on your own terms. That's HUGE!**

4 GOLDEN RULES

- *Always keep a budget*
- *Think of savings as a monthly cost*
- *Never spend more than you earn*
- *Invest (wisely)*

"You don't have to see the whole staircase, just take the first step."
-Martin Luther King Jr.

STEP 1: *Save as much as you can*

STEP 2: *Grow your savings*

All Legendary Adults know there are two key ways to grow wealth...

Compound Interest

This is the key to extreme wealth, often referred to as 'interest on interest'. Wherever you put your money, you want the highest compounding interest rate, which means you earn interest on the initial money (the principal), and then more interest on the principal plus the initial interest, continuing on until potentially you are earning more interest on previous interest than the principal itself! It's like free money! Your money is growing without you doing a thing, and the bigger the principal, the bigger the return. Usually the higher the interest rate the higher the risk... but more on that later.

Asset Value Growth

An asset is something of value that you own and could sell for money. The idea is that over time the value of that thing will increase. Properties have traditionally been this kind of investment, where the asset (the house) is purchased for a cost, but the value of the asset (hopefully) goes up over time. If the house were sold, whatever extra the owner would earn after accounting for the original cost of the house is called the return on investment (ROI). Once you sell an asset you are charged tax on the ROI (unless the asset is your primary residence).

This is the same idea when you invest in other kinds of assets like company stocks. Imagine having bought 100 stocks from a world-renowned company back when one stock cost $25, and today each one is worth $25,000. This kind of thing really happens! Usually it takes some time though (think 20+ years), but it goes to show that making smart decisions now can make your future a whole lot brighter.

SAVINGS CHALLENGE
$10,000 IN 52 WEEKS!

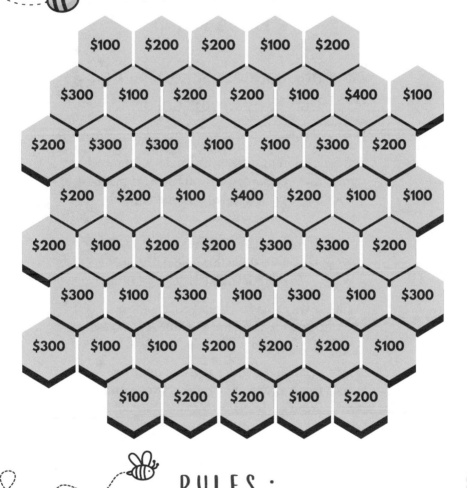

$100	$200	$200	$100	$200

$300 $100 $200 $200 $100 $400 $100

$200 $300 $300 $100 $100 $300 $200

$200 $200 $100 $400 $200 $100 $100

$200 $100 $200 $200 $300 $300 $200

$300 $100 $300 $100 $300 $100 $300

$300 $100 $100 $200 $200 $200 $100

$100 $200 $200 $100 $200

RULES :

Cut out this page and stick it on the wall.

Start with any amount, no need to go sequentially.

Every time you save, cross out the nominal on the honeycomb.

Get That Honey!

WANNA BUY SOMETHING EXPENSIVE?

For Goodness Sake, Don't Use Your Credit Card!*

You should still save money even if you don't have a goal in mind. But if you do, a financial goal tracker (like the one on the next page) can help break it down into manageable chunks.

You could enter the amounts and dates you want to make 'deposits' ahead of time or write it in as you go.

Either way this will help you see the goal clearly when it's laid out in front of you, and help you hold yourself accountable.

If it's a purchase under say, $2,000.00, save cash. Get a jar, an envelope, whatever, and only store savings for this specific goal in there.

*By all means... use your card, just pay it off right away!

Pro Tip

Since you have a credit card anyway, make it work for you! Find one that has benefits you can use, whether it's for travel, dividends, or more points at a store you always go to. Use your card for everything to rack up the benefits, just make sure you pay it off either as you go or at the end of each month.

SAVINGS GOAL

Goal:

Date	Amount

Start Date:

Deadline:

Total:

SAVINGS GOAL

Goal:

Date	Amount

Start Date:

Deadline:

Total:

THE No-Spend CHALLENGE

Step One: Lock up those credit cards, hide the cash, and let your savings breathe a sigh of relief. Choose a specific timeframe, whether it's a day, a week, or a month, and avoid any spending unless it's a necessity.

Step Two: Get creative with meal planning, raid the pantry like a culinary ninja, and turn leftovers into gourmet delights.

Step Three: Say "goodbye" to online shopping temptations and "hello" to DIY projects that make your wallet thank you.

Step Four: Embrace the freebies, from library books to outdoor adventures. Who needs pricey entertainment when you've got nature's playground?

Step Five: Celebrate your newfound frugality with an adulting-victory dance, and watch your savings pile up!

How To Invest

The goal of investing is to grow your money, and there are a lot of ways to do it. A popular and traditional method is purchasing real estate or other physical assets. The other main way people invest money is through the stock market, and there are many different methods to do so. We'll review the basic ones here.

Real Estate

Investing in real estate generally means buying and leveraging property. Real estate value tends to appreciate (go up) over time, but it takes a lot of research, work, and smart decisions to maximize profits. Another way of investing in real estate is by purchasing REITs on the stock market (more on that later).

Retirement Savings Plans

These are tax-advantaged retirement savings accounts, like a 401k or IRA in the USA, or an RRSP or TFSA in Canada. There are may be restrictions around how much money you can deposit and when you can take money out of these accounts. The great thing is you can hold assets like stocks in these accounts, and any income generated from those assets is either never taxed, or only taxed upon withdrawal. This means you can save money now and withdraw it when you're retired and pay tax at a lower tax rate. Plus, money deposited into some of these accounts is tax deductible.

Risk !!!

Any kind of investing comes with its own risk, so it's critical to do your homework before you take the plunge. That said, some investments come with higher or lower risk. It's best to keep the largest portion of your investments in something stable with less risk but some growth opportunity. One idea is to earmark a small portion of your investment money to put into higher risk investments for potentially higher profit. Here are 3 key points to always keep in mind:

1. Diversify
2. The higher the potential return, the higher the risk
3. Be prepared to lose sometimes.

Diversify Your Portfolio - This is the number one way of reducing your risk and increasing your opportunity for growth. Owning a bunch of different kinds of stocks and assets means if one loses value, it's only a small fraction of your total wealth. Diversifying also means you have exposure to many markets (like green energy, banking, AI, etc... all very different), some of which will do better than others at different times. Diversity also means you're more likely to benefit when any given market does go through the roof.

THE STOCK MARKET

The world of stocks can be overwhelming. Understanding the basic types of stocks listed below, and a few other terms and concepts, will make things slightly less terrifying.

Traditionally, and still today, many people use Portfolio Managers through a bank or a private investment company to purchase, manage, and often choose your stocks and assets. These days many others choose online platforms that allow you total control of your portfolio. Fees are charged for any trade (purchase or sale of a stock) which depends on the platform or bank, and which exchange the stock is listed on.

STOCKS

Stocks are tiny pieces of a company listed on a stock exchange that anyone can purchase. The company sells these pieces to generate money to invest back into the company in order to gain more profit. This profit is then shared with you, the shareholder, when hopefully the price of the stock increases.

DIVIDEND STOCKS

Dividend Stocks are regular stocks that also pay the shareholder a dividend, a cash amount on a monthly or quarterly basis. This can be reinvested to compound, or withdrawn as passive income. These stocks tend not to grow much in value (unlike 'growth stocks' which have no dividend), but can make up for it in the overall return.

Investment Funds

Teams of investment brokers pool clients' money to create funds, which buy and trade various stocks and assets. There are a lot of benefits to owning funds rather than individual stocks, and you can buy pieces of these funds just like you would buy a stock. Funds are managed by professionals who make decisions on what to buy and any trading strategies used to gain profit. These funds do come with annual fees, called the Management Expense Ratio (MER). It's calculated as a percentage of your fund assets. Here are a few common types of investment funds:

MUTUAL FUNDS

These are funds that hold a wide variety of stocks, bonds and other assets. They are generally lower risk than other types of investments. Banks or investment brokers often offer a choice between low, medium, and high risk mutual funds. The lower the risk, the lower the return. Mutual funds are usually held on a long-term basis.

REITS

REITs or Real Estate Investment Trusts are funds that own real estate assets like commercial properties, warehouses, hospitals, residential properties, even infrastructure like renewable energy projects or toll roads. It's a good way to invest in real estate without the need for a giant down payment to purchase a rental property, let alone the stress of managing it!

ETFS

ETFs or Exchange-Traded Funds hold a variety of different stocks and assets, and many ETFs are actually index funds. It's easy to find ETFs that cater to a specific area of the market that suits your values or interests. Some even pay a nice dividend. ETFs' MER is usually lower than mutual funds' MERs because they are not as actively managed.

What Else Can You Buy On The Stock Market?

BONDS

Bonds are like IOUs issued by governments, cities, or companies when they need to borrow money. When you buy a bond, you're lending money to the issuer, and in return, they promise to pay you back the amount you lent (the principal) at a later date, along with periodic interest payments.

CURRENCIES

Forex refers to the global market where currencies are traded against each other, for instance the exchange of US dollars for euros or Japanese yen. It is the largest and most liquid (meaning cash) financial market in the world, with participants including banks, corporations, governments, and individual traders.

COMMODITIES

Commodities are raw materials or primary agricultural products that are traded on commodity exchanges, such as gold, oil, wheat, and coffee. Investors often trade commodities to diversify their portfolios..

STOCK EXCHANGES

Stock exchanges are financial marketplaces where buyers and sellers trade shares of publicly listed companies. Countries with a stable financial system usually have their own exchange, or several exchanges catering to specific areas of the market. You can trade on any exchange, depending on what is available through your investment broker or platform.

The two biggest stock exchanges are in the USA, The New York Stock Exchange (NYSE) and the NASDAQ (which caters to the tech market). Canada has the Toronto Stock Exchange (TSX), and Tokyo (TSE), Shanghai (SSE), and Hong Kong (HKEX) have their own exchanges too. The London Stock Exchange (LSE) is the one of the oldest and most prestigious exchanges in international finance.

Stock Indexes

Stock Indices are like scoreboards that measure the performance of a group of stocks. They are meant to represent the overall performance of a particular market or a specific segment of it. For example, the S&P 500 Index tracks the performance of the 500 largest companies listed on stock exchanges in the United States.

Index Funds

Stock index funds are investment funds that aim to replicate the performance of a specific stock index. Instead of trying to pick individual stocks, these funds invest in the same stocks that make up the index they're tracking.

Terms To Know

Blue Chip Stocks

Stocks of well-established companies with a history of stable earnings, strong financials, and reliability. They are considered relatively safe investments and are often core holdings in investment portfolios.

Wall Street

Wall Street is an actual street in New York City that is home to the New York Stock Exchange. It has become synonymous with the financial market in the United States.

Volatility

volatility means how much the price of something goes up and down. If something has high volatility, its price changes a lot over time. High volatility can mean bigger chances for both gains and losses, while low volatility means more predictability.

Portfolio

This is a person or institution's collection of assets. The goal of a portfolio is to achieve a balance between risk and return by diversifying investments across different asset classes and sectors.

Ticker Symbol

Companies each have one to identify it on an exchange (MSFT=Microsoft)

Bull vs Bear Markets

You'll hear people refer to the stock market as Bullish or Bearish at any given time depending on whether profits are trending up (Bullish - a bull swipes up with his horns) or trending down (Bearish - a bear swipes down with it's paws).

The market goes through cycles, and historically-speaking, inevitably moves in an overall upward trend. This doesn't go for all stocks though! Many individual companies end up failing or simply losing market value and never gain it back.

Buy The Dips!

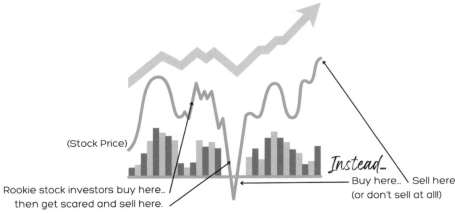

(Stock Price)

Rookie stock investors buy here...
then get scared and sell here.

Instead...
Buy here... Sell here
(or don't sell at all!)

Do you see the problem?

Smart investors understand that bear markets and market dips are opportunities in disguise. By holding onto stocks during downturns and even buying more at discounted prices, they position themselves for long-term wealth growth. These strategic moves not only capitalize on market fluctuations but also demonstrate resilience in the face of uncertainty.

It's a game-changer, turning potential losses into gains and shaping the trajectory of your financial future. In the world of investing, embracing market dips can truly make or break a person's wealth journey.

Happy Investing!

of INVESTING

- ⬤ Diversify your portfolio
- ⬤ Stay patient for long-term gains
- ⬤ Invest without research
- ⬤ Reinvest dividends
- ⬤ Panic-sell during market dips
- ⬤ Put all your money in one stock
- ⬤ Go into debt to invest

Help this nice couple navigate through the labyrinth that is the banking system to get a loan for their first home.

Watch out for those 'consultants' along the way. Don't get lured in by their bad advice!

How BANKING
Really Works

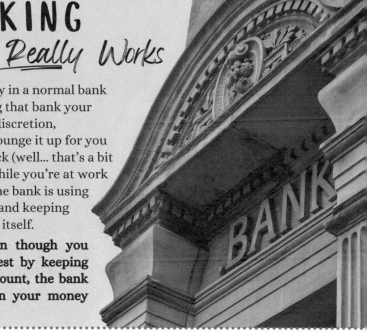

By keeping your money in a normal bank account, you are giving that bank your money to use at their discretion, as long as they can scrounge it up for you when you ask for it back (well... that's a bit complicated too). So while you're at work earning those bucks, the bank is using your money to invest, and keeping 99.9% of the profits for itself.

This means that even though you may gain some interest by keeping your money in an account, the bank will earn far more on your money than you do.

This is important to know, but don't let it stop you from using banks. Just be wary, as you should when dealing with any large corporation or institution. The capitalist system is INTENDED to take advantage of the little guys - you and me. The first step to avoid this is to GAIN KNOWLEDGE. The second step is to use the same methods the banks do and make your money work for you too.

FINANCIAL ADVISORS
Not all financial advisors are created equal. Do your research!

The term 'Financial Advisor' refers to someone who works for a financial institution and has a relevant background including certification in financial planning. At the very least they require specialized financial planning courses and need to be licensed by a regulatory body. These people can help guide your financial decisions, but make sure you find the right person...

Fiduciary Duty: While not mandated by law yet in North America, there is an increasing emphasis on advisors to act in the best interests of their clients, referred to as a fiduciary duty. Some professional organizations set fiduciary standards and codes of ethics (as they should) which some advisors voluntarily adhere to. However, Financial Advisors are motivated to sell certain products over others based on a better commission for themselves, so many avoid such standards and simply don't always act in their clients best interests. Such is the corporate reality.

BEWARE! Banks and institutions have many job titles that sound like Financial Advisor but require zero training or qualification. Be careful when getting advice from a "Financial Consultant", "Personal Banker", or "Wealth Management Associate".

Cryptocurrency

Bitcoin, the first cryptocurrency, was created in 2008. It is a global peer-to-peer electronic cash system which eliminates the need for intermediaries like banks. By using algorithms and cryptography to maintain security, cryptocurrency is completely decentralized and anonymous. Whereas Big Banks can access the money you keep with them, invest it for their own returns, and control it in other ways as well, this can't happen with cryptocurrency.

Since the release of Bitcoin, many other such "currencies" have been created, called Altcoins, Etherium being the most popular.

"WHEN IT COMES TO CRYPTOCURRENCY, NEVER INVEST MORE THAN YOU CAN AFFORD TO LOSE"

People invest in crypto by buying Bitcoin or other cryptocurrencies which, just like stocks or regular ("fiat") currencies, can increase or decrease in value. Think of cryptocurrency as the Wild West of the financial world. It's still very new and as such it's also still unregulated. This makes for a lot of risk but a lot of potential reward.

The crypto world has a ton of terms you'll need to know. We've listed some of them here.

Investing in cryptocurrency requires serious research and knowledge, so make sure you adult it, and do your due diligence ahead of time!

Key Terms

Blockchain: A distributed digital ledger that records all transactions across a network of computers. It is the underlying technology of most cryptocurrencies.

Cryptocurrency: A digital or virtual currency that uses cryptography for security and operates on decentralized networks.

Bitcoin (BTC): The first and most well-known cryptocurrency, created by an unknown person or group of people using the pseudonym Satoshi Nakamoto.

Altcoin: Any cryptocurrency other than Bitcoin (ex. Ethereum (ETH), Ripple (XRP), Litecoin (LTC), and many others).

Wallet: A digital or physical tool that allows users to store, send, and receive cryptocurrencies.

Centralized / Decentralized Exchange: Centralized exchanges are platforms where users trade digital assets like crypto through a central authority, relying on the exchange to manage funds and execute transactions. Decentralized exchanges operate without a central authority, allowing users to trade directly from their digital wallets, offering increased privacy and control over their assets.

Private or Public Keys: Passwords used to access and control the activities of a crypto wallet, including sending and receiving cryptocurrency transactions.

Mining: The process by which new cryptocurrency coins are created and transactions are added to the blockchain. It involves solving complex mathematical problems.

Cryptocurrency Exchange: An online platform where users can buy, sell, and trade cryptocurrencies.

Decentralized Finance (DeFi): Financial services built on blockchain technology in order to operate without traditional intermediaries like banks.

Improve Your Financial Situation

Always spend less than you earn

Have multiple sources of income

Do your research before making big financial decisions

Prioritize Savings

Create and maintain an emergency fund

Draw a personal financial roadmap for the next five years (at least!)

DEBT
Destroyer of Wealth

Debt is when you borrow money from a person, institution (like a bank), or entity with the agreement to pay it back later. This borrowed money is typically used for various purposes, such as making purchases, paying bills, or investing in something.

Interest is the additional fee charged for the service of borrowing money. The lender charges interest as a percentage of the total amount you borrow. The interest rate is determined based on various factors like the type of loan, the lender's policies, and your credit score.

How Debt and Interest Work Together: When you borrow money, you agree to repay the original amount (the principal) plus the interest over a specific period.

A Simple Loan:
If you take out a loan for $1,000.00 at a 5% annual interest rate, you'll owe the lender $1,050.00 at the end of the year (the $1,000.00 principal plus $50.00 in interest).

A Mortgage:
For a mortgage with a home price of $500,000.00, a 10% down payment of $50,000.00, and an interest rate of 5%, the total principal borrowed would be $450,000.00. Then you would also pay an additional $420,600.00 in interest over a term of 30 years ... a grand total of $870,000.00.

Pro Tip
Avoid building up credit card debt at all cost! Credit cards usually have an interest rate of 20% or more!

COMPOUNDING DEBT

Bye Bye Money...

Compounding debt is when interest accrues not just on the principal, but also on the accumulated interest that has not been paid. As interest builds up, it gets added to the outstanding balance, becoming part of the new principal. This results in interest being charged on both the original borrowed sum and the previously built up interest, causing the debt to grow exponentially over time. Without consistent payments that cover both the interest and a portion of the principal, compounding debt can lead to a substantial increase in what you owe.

THE CATCH-22 OF BORROWING

In today's society, debt is something of a necessary evil. For example, most people don't have the ability to save up enough to buy a property outright, but owning one has traditionally been an investment that improves your financial situation in the long run. Therefore it may be wise to take out a loan out for a large purchase like that. Taking on debt responsibly is also necessary to develop a good credit score, and having a good credit score is essential.

On the flip side, taking on debt that you can't realistically manage will devastate your financial situation and WILL result in the black hole of compounding debt (as well as a terrible credit score).

CREDIT SCORE

Credit scores are partly determined by how well individuals manage credit and debt. Build up your credit score by taking on small amounts of debt like a credit card. Here's how to manage it effectively:

- Always pay more than the minimum payment required
- Never miss or make a late payment on any bill
- Figure out a healthy utilization rate (using the debt enough, but always leaving part of it unused, at least 10%)
- Avoid payday loans, cash advances, and other high-risk, high-interest loans AT ALL COST!

TO BORROW... OR NOT TO BORROW...

Good Reasons

You have worked hard to save a downpayment on a property and need a mortgage from the bank. You also know you will have enough income to manage and pay back the loan over time.

You want to pursue an education and have a chosen field in mind which you know has opportunities for new graduates. (Yes, you researched this too).

You have a long-term plan for purchasing a house, and have been advised by (a genuine) Financial Advisor to improve your credit score which is low because you have no credit history.

Terrible, Bad, No-Good Reasons

Because every month you spend more than you earn (BAD BAD VERY BAD!!)

Because that designer bag is on sale and it's ONLY $4,500.00.

Because you spent the money you saved for the trip to Cuba on a new wardrobe... for the trip to Cuba.

Because Sophia is acting weird but maybe she'll be impressed if you show up in a new ride.

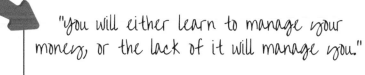

"you will either learn to manage your money, or the lack of it will manage you."

Dave Ramsey

Did You Know...

Cleaning your home isn't just a chore, it can be a
full-body workout disguised as household tasks.
A person burns around 250-350 calories per hour
while cleaning. Who needs a gym membership?

Cleaning
Yes, You Must!

You know what they say, cleanliness is next to godliness. Your home is your sanctuary and now that you're the boss, it's up to you to keep the place in decent shape. Any adult will tell you it's true that the state of your home reflects the state of your mind, and that it's hard to focus on life's priorities when your home's a mess.

But let's be real, cleaning sucks. So read on for some tips and tricks and easy-to-follow to-do lists, to help cleaning up feel like a breeze.

CLEANING SUPPLIES TO KEEP ON HAND

- ALL-PURPOSE CLEANING SPRAY
- WINDOW CLEANING SPRAY
- GENERAL PURPOSE CLEANER (CONCENTRATED)
- BAKING SODA
- CELLULOSE SPONGES (WITH AN ABRASIVE SIDE)
- STAINLESS STEEL CLEANING PADS
- MICROFIBRE CLOTHS
- MELAMINE SPONGE
- EMPTY SPRAY BOTTLE
- DISHSOAP
- LAUNDRY DETERGENT
- BROOM & DUSTPAN
- MOP & BUCKET
- OLD TOOTHBRUSH
(FOR SCRUBBING BETWEEN TILES, GROUT, AND AROUND FAUCETS)

Typical cleaners use hazardous ingredients that can actually damage some surfaces and send poisonous chemicals into the water system.

Check out page 79 on how to be an environmentally conscious cleaner and make your own natural disinfectants which are way better for you and the planet.

Did You Know:

A study on young adults found that clutter was linked to procrastination, feeling overwhelmed and a lower quality of life.

Melamine Sponges are the generic version of the so-called "Cleaning Eraser" which is "Magic" (they're white and look like a giant eraser) ...and magic they are, my friend!

Use them on walls or other grimy places with hard to clean stains, film, or other gunk.

Definitely a Pro Adulting item!

ERASER

BENEFITS OF CLEANING YOUR HOME

REDUCES STRESS

Stress can be triggered by a messy environment. which can lead to feeling overwhelmed.

IMPROVES FOCUS

A clean environment helps you to be more focused and work more effectively.

BOOSTS YOUR MOOD

Research shows that a clean and tidy home will help to boost your mood. Let's start cleaning!

CHECKLIST

Not everything needs to be cleaned every day... thank goodness!
Use this checklist to guide you, or create your own with the blank
template on the next page.

DAILY

- [ ] Tidy Up
- [ ] Make Your Bed
- [ ] Wash Dishes
- [ ] Spot Sweet
- [ ] Wipe Kitchen Counters

WEEKLY

- [ ] Dust All Surfaces
- [ ] Vacuum carpets
- [ ] Clean Windows
- [ ] Do Laundry
- [ ] Clean Microwave
- [ ] Take Out The Garbage
- [ ] Clean Bathrooms
- [ ] Change Bedsheets
- [ ] Sanitize Surfaces
- [ ] Sweep & Mop Floors

MONTHLY

- [ ] Declutter
- [ ] Wipe Down Kitchen Cabinets
- [ ] Scrub Stove & Burners
- [ ] Clean Bedroom
- [ ] Clean The Fridge (In & Out)
- [ ] Tidy Up Storage And Cabinets
- [ ] Sweep & Mop Behind Furniture
- [ ] Vacuum Couches & Upholstery
- [ ] Wipe Down Baseboards
- [ ] Clean The Tub & Shower
- [ ] Spot Clean Walls
- [ ] Clean Oven
  (Many ovens have a self-clean function)

YEARLY

- [ ] Change Smoke Alarm Batteries
- [ ] Clean Out Kitchen Cupboards
- [ ] Clean Bathroom Cabinets
- [ ] Clean Out Junk Drawers
- [ ] Clean Out Closet & Donate Old Items
- [ ] Clean Outside Windows

Cleaning
CHECKLIST

Not everything needs to be cleaned every day... thank goodness!
Use this checklist to guide you, or create your own with the blank
template on the next page.

DAILY

- [ ] Tidy Up
- [ ] Wash Dishes
- [ ] Wipe Kitchen Counters
- [ ] Make Your Bed
- [ ] Spot Sweet

WEEKLY

- [ ] Dust All Surfaces
- [ ] Clean Windows
- [ ] Clean Microwave
- [ ] Clean Bathrooms
- [ ] Sanitize Surfaces
- [ ] Vacuum Carpets
- [ ] Do Laundry
- [ ] Take Out The Garbage
- [ ] Change Bedsheets
- [ ] Sweep & Mop Floors

MONTHLY

- [ ] Declutter
- [ ] Scrub Stove & Burners
- [ ] Clean The Fridge (In & Out)
- [ ] Sweep & Mop Behind Furniture
- [ ] Wipe Down Baseboards
- [ ] Spot Clean Walls
- [ ] Wipe Down Kitchen Cabinets
- [ ] Clean Bedroom
- [ ] Tidy Up Storage And Cabinets
- [ ] Vacuum Couches & Upholstery
- [ ] Clean The Tub & Shower
- [ ] Clean Oven
  (Many ovens have a self-clean function)

YEARLY

- [ ] Change Smoke Alarm Batteries
- [ ] Clean Bathroom Cabinets
- [ ] Clean Out Closet & Donate Old Items
- [ ] Clean Out Kitchen Cupboards
- [ ] Clean Out Junk Drawers
- [ ] Clean Outside Windows

Cleaning
CHECKLIST

DAILY

- [ ] ----------------------------------
- [ ] ----------------------------------
- [ ] ----------------------------------

- [ ] ----------------------------------
- [ ] ----------------------------------
- [ ] ----------------------------------

WEEKLY

- [ ] ----------------------------------
- [ ] ----------------------------------
- [ ] ----------------------------------
- [ ] ----------------------------------
- [ ] ----------------------------------

- [ ] ----------------------------------
- [ ] ----------------------------------
- [ ] ----------------------------------
- [ ] ----------------------------------
- [ ] ----------------------------------

MONTHLY

- [ ] ----------------------------------
- [ ] ----------------------------------
- [ ] ----------------------------------
- [ ] ----------------------------------
- [ ] ----------------------------------
- [ ] ----------------------------------

- [ ] ----------------------------------
- [ ] ----------------------------------
- [ ] ----------------------------------
- [ ] ----------------------------------
- [ ] ----------------------------------
- [ ] ----------------------------------

YEARLY

- [ ] ----------------------------------
- [ ] ----------------------------------
- [ ] ----------------------------------
- [ ] ----------------------------------

- [ ] ----------------------------------
- [ ] ----------------------------------
- [ ] ----------------------------------
- [ ] ----------------------------------

Cleaning
CHECKLIST

DAILY

- ☐ -----------------
- ☐ -----------------
- ☐ -----------------

- ☐ -----------------
- ☐ -----------------
- ☐ -----------------

WEEKLY

- ☐ -----------------
- ☐ -----------------
- ☐ -----------------
- ☐ -----------------
- ☐ -----------------

- ☐ -----------------
- ☐ -----------------
- ☐ -----------------
- ☐ -----------------
- ☐ -----------------

MONTHLY

- ☐ -----------------
- ☐ -----------------
- ☐ -----------------
- ☐ -----------------
- ☐ -----------------
- ☐ -----------------

- ☐ -----------------
- ☐ -----------------
- ☐ -----------------
- ☐ -----------------
- ☐ -----------------
- ☐ -----------------

YEARLY

- ☐ -----------------
- ☐ -----------------
- ☐ -----------------
- ☐ -----------------

- ☐ -----------------
- ☐ -----------------
- ☐ -----------------
- ☐ -----------------

ENVIRONMENTALLY CONSCIOUS Cleaning

Cleaning your home using natural products is a great way to keep your home clean while reducing chemical pollution. You can buy natural products at the store (which are a bit pricier), or make your own with stuff you already have at home.

ESSENTIAL OILS

Add your own blend of essential oils to the cleaning products you make. This is what Legendary Adulting smells like!

RECIPES

Always spot-test natural products on surfaces before you clean

All-Purpose Spray

1 cup distilled water
1/4 cup white vinegar
2 tbsp rubbing alcohol
10-15 drops essential oil

Deep Cleaning Paste

Create a paste by mixing baking soda with a little water and use it to scrub surfaces such as sinks, tubs, and grout.

Glass Cleaner

Pour white vinegar into a spray bottle. Pretty simple! Use a cloth or newspaper to wipe it off for streak-free results.

Air & Fabric Deodorizing Spray

1 cup distilled water
2 tbsp witch hazel
10 drops essential oil
1 tsp baking soda

Disinfecting Spray

Mix 1 part hydrogen peroxide with 1 part water for a general disinfectant spray. You can use straight undiluted hydrogen peroxide to disinfect cutting boards, tooth-brushes, sponges, etc.

CASTILLE SOAP

This biodegradable soap made from vegetable oils can be used as dish soap, or dilute it with water to make a general purpose floor and surface cleaner.

CLEANING TIPS & TRICKS

No adulting guide would be complete without a few golden cleaning tricks, the kind you normally figure out after years of putting in more effort than you need to. Not you, my friend! Here's an awesome list of choice tips that will impress even the most seasoned cleaners.

1 Stainless Steel

Dab a little olive oil onto a microfibre cloth and buff stainless steel surfaces in circular motions. The oil leaves a protective shine.

2 Slat Blinds

Wrap microfibre cloths around the arms of a pair of tongs. Over that, wrap two dryer sheets, and secure the covering to each arm with elastic bands. The tongs should still be able to open and close. Grip the sides of the blind with the tongs and wipe off the dust easily. The dryer sheets prevent static, keeping your blinds dust-free longer, and smelling nice!

Don't get your hands dirty while you're checking for the delivery driver for the 10th time

3 Water Stains on Wood

Rub a bit of mayonnaise onto water stains on wood furniture. Let it sit for a few hours or overnight and then wipe off. This helps lift the water and restore the wood's finish.

Thats my couch... you know that right?

4 Hair & Fur

Put on a rubber glove and make it slightly damp. Rub your glove hand over upholstry, clothes, carpets, and other fabric to easily capture stray hairs, fluff and other fibres. Works great for pet hair!

5 Sticker Residue & Glue

Rub cooking oil on any sticky residue that won't wash off with regular cleaner. Let it soak for 10 minutes. It will wipe off easily.

6 Ceiling Fans

Side a pillow case over the fan blade and gently pull it back, trapping all the dust inside. Shake it out into a clean garbage bag and repeat for the other blades. You can wipe them again with a microfibre cloth to get them perfectly dust-free.

7 Microwave

Steam clean your microwave by heating water with lemon on high for a few minutes until it is boiling and creating steam. When that's done, leave the door closed for a few minutes. The steam will loosen any hardened food and make it easy to wipe away.

8 Disinfect Sponges

Cellulose sponges trap debris which can lead to bacteria growth. When your sponges start to smell, rather than replace them immediately, disinfect them in the microwave. Rinse the sponge as well as possible and place in the microwave on high for 1-2 minutes.

Pro Tip:

Always place sponges on their sides to dry, never with the cellulose facing down. Proper air drying will reduce any bacteria growth.

9 Dryer Sheets

Dryer sheets are useful to clean with because they reduce static cling which is actually negative ions building up on surfaces. This attracts dust. Dryer sheets have positive ions that neutralize the negative charge. Dryer sheets also have lubricants, plus a nice fragrance. Use them to wipe baseboards and other places where dust builds up quickly.

How To Unclog a Drain

SCENARIO: Your kitchen sink is clogged and full of the grimiest smelliest most sickening liquid substance that you've ever encountered. Fun adulting times! Do you:

a) Seal off the area and order takeout from now on.

b) Use the bathroom sink. Potato peels next to your toothbrush seems normal.

c) Get a wet vac. This is your new drain.

d) Try a plunger, a snake tool, or a chemical agent (in that order).

PLUNGER

1) Invest in a good one! Find one with a wide thick lip, made of thick rubber. Dollarstore plungers will not do!

2) Scoop out as much water/muck as possible from the sink.

3) Place the mouth of the plunger over the drain to make a seal. Push hard straight down towards the drain, and pull up. Repeat until the suction works to loosen the gunk. Careful, gross stuff might come flying out!

DRAIN SNAKE

This is basically a coiled wire with some hooks on the end. Works better than a coat hanger. Buying a good quality one will make this easier.

1) Scoop out as much water and gunk as you can.

2) Send the hook end down the drain as far as possible. Turn the top end and keep forcing the hooks down so they can grab onto the blockage and loosen it.

CHEMICAL AGENT

Make this your last resort before calling your landlord or a plumber since it does send nasty chemicals into the water system.

Look in the cleaning aisles at your local hardware or grocery store for various drain deglogging agents.

Follow instructions on the bottle.

STAIN REMOVAL GUIDE

Even Legendary Adults spill their coffee on their white shirts (shhh!), they just know how to clean it properly. Hydrogen Peroxide, Rubbing Alcohol, Cornstarch, Baking Soda, Salt, and Bleach are key to handling any stain.

STAIN REMOVAL PASTE RECIPE:

Mix together 1 tbsp each:
- Hydrogen Peroxide
- Salt
- Baking Soda

Apply paste and let it sit before gently scrubbing.

Coffe / Tea

Soak in cool water. Pretreat with a prewash spray, a liquid laundry detergent, or a paste of detergent and water. Launder with chlorine bleach, if safe for the fabric

Blood

Soak the stain in cold water as soon as possible. If the stain is super fresh, place it under cold running water first. Sponge the stain with hydrogen peroxide, or rub bar soap into the stain. Launder with bleach if possible.

Sweat Stains

Soak clothing in a solution of white vinegar and water, then applying a stain removal paste (see recipe above). Allow the mixture to rest, scrub the stain with an old toothbrush and machine wash in hot water.

Grass

Mix one part distilled white vinegar with one part water. Coat the stain, let sit (30 minutes or so), scrub, and rinse in cool water. Then repeat the same steps with the detergent: scrub, sit, and rinse.

Lipstick, Cosmetics

Apply rubbing alcohol to a cotton ball or clean cloth and dab (don't rub) the stain away. Repeat until the lipstick color is removed. Wash according to care instructions.

Grease

Apply a big scoop of cornstarch to a grease stain on a piece of clothing and allow it to sit for 12 hours. Then proceed with washing it normally.

PLANTS...

THE ORIGINAL 100% NATURAL, SOLAR-POWERED, FILTERLESS, BPA-FREE

AIR PURIFIER!

It's the OG way to lower levels of indoor pollutants and minimize your exposure to harmful compounds in the air. How Adult of you! You know how trees take in carbon dioxide and give off oxygen? Yeah... little ones can do it too... in your own house!

Plus, they look really cool, and can double as a christmas tree in a pinch... pro-tip right there.

Keep in mind not all plants are the same. Some like bright sun, some hate it. Some die in sandy soil, some thrive in it. So (as always), plan ahead and do your research! Now that's adulting.

Top 3 *Air-Purifying Plants*

RUBBER TREE

SNAKE PLANT

ALOE VERA

Pro Tip
Got a cut? Sunburn? Rash? Acne? Snap off a piece of Aloe Vera and rub the gel right onto your skin.

REMEMBER: IF YOU WANT YOUR PLANTS TO TAKE CARE OF YOU, YOU NEED TO TAKE CARE OF THEM TOO!

If your indoor plants are sad, consider the following:

Overwatering or Underwatering: Research how much water the type of plant prefers. As a general rule, water enough that all the soil in the pot will be damp but not enough to pool at the bottom. Only water again when the top 1-2 inches of soil is bone dry.

Light: Think about the location of the plant and how much sun it gets throughout the day. Most indoor tropical plants do well with indirect or "dappled" sunlight, as this is what it's like in their natural environment. This is great for apartments or areas with less sunlight. If it's a really dark corner find a plant that wants little to no direct sun.

Humidity: In tropical forests humidity is way higher than in our homes. Dry air can cause issues for us and our plants, so think of getting a humidifier or putting a diffuser near the plant.

Soil: You can buy specialized soil, or you can amend normal garden soil which means adding nutrients and materials that help the plant to thrive.

Changes: Plants get shocked too if something changes suddenly, and if it does you'll notice. Maybe the plant's new location is close to a window where it's too cold or there's more sun than the plant is used to.

Location: This really takes all of the above into consideration. It's thinking about the details like light sources, how warm you keep your place, and how close the plant is to sources of heat, cold, and air.

Plants want your scraps!

NATURAL FERTILIZER RECIPE
Coffee Grounds (1 cup, dry)
Banana Peels (2-3 whole or cut up)
Egg Shells (from 4-5 eggs, airdried)

1. Blend ingredients until coarse. Transfer to a bucket and stir in 2L of water. Leave for 3 days to steep, stirring every so often.
2. Use fine mesh strainer or cheesecloth to strain the liquid. Discard the solid stuff left over.
3. Use this concentrated fertilizer by diluting it in water (1:3 ratio- 1 part fertilizer, 3 parts water). Use this to water your plants, making sure it doesn't come in contact with the leaves.
4. Store in an air-tight container in a cool dry place. Use within a few weeks.

BINGO

Adult In The Kitchen
Edition

Burnt the leftovers	Earring down the kitchen sink	Left the oven on... again	Unknown substance in tupperware	Left the milk out overnight
Single withered carrot in the veggie drawer	Mysterious stench of unknown origin	Chicken looks perfect. It's also frozen in the middle	Opened the fridge ...forgot why	Honey spilled in the cupboard
6 year old salad dressing in the fridge	Start a recipe, but missing ingredients	Watered the plants with hot tap water... oops	Moldy cereal bowls	Mystery sauce without a label or expiry date
Frozen popsicle juice in the freezer	Eating dinner out of tupperware	Microwave Explosion	Garbage juice at the bottom of the bin	Burning sugar smells bad!
Grease drips on the walls	Missed garbage day... not good	Oven mitt has a hole	Not enough dishes for the guests	Used salt instead of sugar

How many of these fun adulting-in-the-kitchen fails have you had yet? Give yourself a prize if you get five in a row. Bingo! welcome to the club...
It's all part of the course towards Legendary Adulthood!

FOOD

You don't need to spend your college years eating Ramen noodles!

Pro Tip

Make your meal plans at the same time you write your grocery list.

Our Meal Planner has both on one page.

Plan meals that use some of the same ingredients so nothing is wasted at the end of the week.

Food doesn't mean cookies and chocolate anymore. Okay okay, it still does sometimes. But you're an adult now! You know that what you eat determines how you feel, which determines what you do, which determines your overall success. This is serious adulting stuff.

Whether it's bringing a dish to a potluck, cooking a romantic dinner, or just keeping yourself healthy, a real adult has a plan.

From planning, to shopping, to cooking, to what the heck you need to keep on hand... the next few pages have you covered.

Did You Know...

Experts are shifting away from the old food pyramid as the best nutrition model. Instead, everyone is now recommended to portion their plate **1/2 Veg, 1/4 Protein, 1/4 Whole Grain.**

KITCHEN HACKS

Tomato-based recipes may be a bit tart. Simply add a half teaspoon of sugar (or more to your liking) to reduce the acidity.

Cutting onions? Just rub a lemon slice or pre-bought lemon juice on the cutting board. No more tears!

Ground beef recipe? Try replacing a portion with ground pork for a (cheaper) juicier more flavourful result.

Peel garlic in seconds, just put the cloves in a jar, close it up and shake. Perfectly peeled garlic without the garlicky fingers.

Keep brown sugar soft by putting a slice of apple or bread in the bag.

Keep herbs fresh longer by trimming the ends and keeping them in a glass of water. A herb bouquet!

Next time. you over salt a soup or stew, throw in a few raw pieces of apple or potato. Simmer for 10 minutes and discard to remove some of the salt.

KITCHEN CHECKLIST
Stuff Adults Have In Their Kitchens

BASIC COOKING TOOLS

- [ ] Cast Iron Pan with Lid
- [ ] Large Stainless Steel Pot
- [ ] Small Stainless Steel Pot
- [ ] Strainer
- [ ] 2 Large mixing bowls
- [ ] Ladle
- [ ] Slotted Spoon
- [ ] 2 Spatulas (1 hard, 1 soft)
- [ ] Whisk
- [ ] 2 Cooking/ Serving Spoons
- [ ] Bread Knife
- [ ] Chef's Knife
- [ ] Paring Knife
- [ ] Baking Sheet
- [ ] Measuring Cups
- [ ] Measuring Spoons
- [ ] Cheese Grater
- [ ] 2 Cutting Boards
- [ ] Potato Peeler
- [ ] 2 Large Serving Bowls
- [ ] 2 Large Serving Plates
- [ ] Oven Mitts
- [ ] Glass Baking Dish

With these basic tools you'll have everything you need to cook almost anything.

These more 'advanced' tools below will give you an edge on adulting in the kitchen.

PRO ADULT TOOLS

- [ ] Meat Thermometer
- [ ] Steak Knives
- [ ] Basting / Pastry Brush
- [ ] Baking Rack
- [ ] Rolling Pin
- [ ] Tongs
- [ ] Potato Masher
- [ ] Garlic Press
- [ ] Morter & Pestle
- [ ] Filet Knife
- [ ] Cake and Loaf Pans

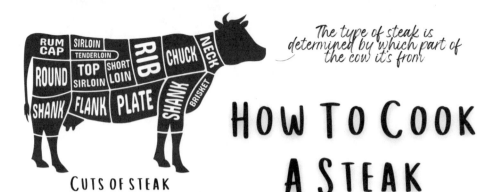

CUTS OF STEAK

HOW TO COOK A STEAK

Ribeye $$$: With rich marbling, the ribeye is a flavourful and tender cut.

Filet Mignon $$$: Super tender, the filet mignon is a lean cut with a buttery texture and mild favour. Prone to drying out if overcooked because it has less fat. Cut thick and round.

New York Strip / Striploin $$$: Balancing tenderness and robust flavour, the New York strip is a versatile and popular choice. Usually boneless.

T-Bone / Porterhouse $$$: This cut features both the tenderloin and strip steak, providing a dual taste experience with a tender portion and a more substantial, well-marbled side. The T-shaped bone adds flavour to the steak. Porterhouse is T-Bone's big brother.

Sirloin $$: A leaner option, sirloin steak is known for its bold beefy flavour and less marbling. Another challenging but rewarding steak to cook well.

Flank Steak $: While not as tender as some other cuts, flank steak is prized for its intense beef flavor and is often used in dishes like fajitas or stir-fries.

Skirt Steak $: With rich flavour and coarse texture, this cut absorbs marinades wonderfully and is great for grilling.

Rare Medium-Rare Medium Medium-Well Well Done

Anyone can grill, but pan-frying a tender juicy steak? That's next level adulting.

PREP

- Use a thick cut (1 - 1.5 inches) The thinner the cut the easier it is to overcook. Skirt or flank steaks will only need 2-3 minutes on each side.

- Before seasoning take the steaks out of the fridge and pat them dry with paper towel.

- Season first with salt on both sides and let it rest uncovered in the fridge for 30 minutes. This will help dry the outside to create a nice crust on the steak and seal in the juices.

- Take the steak out and let it sit semi-covered until it's room temperature (another 30 minutes or so).

- Finally, season the steaks with pepper on both sides.

YOU WILL NEED

Raw steak
2 tbsp vegetable oil
2 tbsp butter
pepper
salt

STEP 1: Heat a skillet with vegetable oil (2 tbsp per steak) on medium-high heat. ONLY add the steak when the oil is shimmering just before it starts to smoke.

STEP 2: Cook the steaks on one side for 7 minutes. If the steak has a bone, reduce cooking time by 1 minute. Then add the butter and turn the steaks, swishing them a bit in the melted butter. Baste the top side of the steaks with the rest of the melted butter in the pan.

STEP 3: Cook the steaks for 4-5 more minutes, or until internal temperature reaches 140 degrees F (medium), or more or less depending on how you want it cooked.

A meat thermometer isn't a must, but it definitely helps!

STEP 4: Remove the steaks and let them rest for 5 minutes before cutting into them. Remember when cutting beef, always cut against the grain.

Pair your steak with two sides and a glass of red wine. Gravy is optional. Don't forget the candles!

HERBS & SPICES

The terms "herbs" and "spices" refer to different parts of plants which are used in distinct ways in cooking.

- **Herbs:** Herbs are typically the leaves of plants. They can be fresh or dried and are valued for their aromatic and flavorful qualities. Examples include basil, parsley, and cilantro. Herbs typically have a milder flavor profile, offering freshness and brightness to dishes. They are often added at the end of the cooking process to preserve their delicate flavors.
- **Spices:** Spices can come from various parts of the plant, such as seeds, bark, roots, or fruits. Spices are often dried and ground before use. Examples include cinnamon (bark), cumin (seeds), and ginger (root). Spices tend to have stronger, more concentrated flavors, and they can add depth, heat, sweetness, or complexity to dishes. Many spices are used in the initial stages of cooking to infuse their flavors into the dish.

BEGINNER'S SPICE PANTRY

Parsley, Basil

Oregano, Rosemary, Thyme

Ginger, Garlic Powder

Cinnamon, Cumin

Paprika, chili powder

Pro Tip

To bring out the aromatics from the spices, add them to a bit of oil in hot pan a minute or two BEFORE adding the liquid.

Did You Know...

Cilantro and coriander come from the same plant. Cilantro is the leaf whereas Coriander refers to the dried seeds.

Wine Guide

An expert adult can always be trusted to bring a good wine. Impress even the snobbiest grown-ups with these tips.

Red

Pair with heartier dishes, like red meat and stews. Also dark chocolate!

Serve at room temperature

Reds are generally bolder and heavier than whites. They're known for their dark fruit flavours like berries and plums and often have chocolaty or spicy notes.

Cabernet Souvignon: Bold and Intense

Merlot: Smoother and less intense than Cabernet, notes of red fruit

Pinot Noir: Complex elegant flavour, with earthy or floral tones

Syrah / Shiraz: Bold flavour, with peppery or floral notes

Zinfandel: Notes of ripe jammy fruit with a hint of sweetness

Malbec: Dark fruit flavours with velvety texture

White

Pair with lighter dishes like fish or chicken. A more refreshing choice in warmer weather.

Serve chilled, right from the fridge.

White wines range from 'dry' (tart) to sweet.

Chardonnay: Unoaked is crisp and acidic, Oaked has creamier texture and sweet notes.

Sauvignon Blanc: Refreshing and crisp

Riesling: Range from dry to sweet. Flavors include green apple, peach, apricot, and floral notes.

Pinot Grigio/Gris: Light and crisp with flavors of green apple, pear, and citrus.

Gewürztraminer: Aromatic, flavors of lychee, rose petals, and tropical fruits.

Moscato / Muscat: Aromatic and sweet with intense floral and fruity notes.

FOOD SAFETY
(Wash Your Hands!!)

Ever have a stomach flu for just one or two days? That was a Food Borne Illness, also known as Food Poisoning. You ate something yucky, probably without even knowing. Yeah, it's gross. Luckily it's easy to avoid, just follow a few easy rules. Remember... you can't see them, but these little guys are everywhere!

> We want to make you MISERABLE!

Fridge Storage

Keep your refrigerator at or below 40°F (4°C).

40°F / 4°C

Refrigerate perishable foods within 2 hours of purchase or preparation (or within 1 hour if the temperature is above 90°F or 32°C).

Thawing Food

Thaw foods safely in the refrigerator, in cold water, or in the microwave. Never thaw foods on the counter at room temperature. This leaves food in the 'danger zone', when bacteria multiply the fastest.

DANGER ZONE:
5°F - 60°F / 41°C - 140°C

Pasteurization involves heating a food or beverage (like milk) to a specific temperature for a set period of time and then rapidly cooling it to kill harmful pathogens. Most dairy products are sold pasteurized.

High Risk Foods

- Unpasteurized Dairy Product
- Raw Meat, Fish, & Shellfish
- Pre-Cut Fruit & Vegetables
- Deli Meat
- Sprouts

Avoid Cross-Contamination

- Wash your hands
- No contact between raw meat and other foods
- Use separate cutting boards and cooking tools
- Surfaces should be sanitized regularly
- Store raw meats on the bottom shelf to prevent drips

Food Storage Guide

If something has an expiry date, follow it! It's there for a reason. Otherwise, see below.

	Fridge (Raw)	Fridge (Cooked)	Freezer (Raw)	Freezer (Cooked)
Whole Chicken	1-2 days	3-4 days	9-12 months	4-6 months
Chicken Pieces	1-2 days	3-4 days	9 months	4 months
Ground Meat	1-2 days	3-4 days	3-4 months	2-3 months
Steaks, Chops, Roasts	3-5 days	3-4 days	5-12 months	4-6 months
Fish	1-2 days	3-4 days	6 months	3 months
Shellfish	1-2 days	1-2 days	3 months	3 months
Deli Meat	-	3-5 days	-	1-2 months
Eggs (in shell)	3-5 weeks	1 week	Don't freeze	Don't freeze
Dairy Products	Follow expiry dates, they're there for a reason.		Freezing dairy products and fresh produce is generally not recommended.	
Fresh Produce	If it looks gross, don't eat it!			
Leftovers	-	3-4 days	-	2-3 months

When in Doubt, Throw it Out!

Safe Cooking Temperatures

	Minimum Internal Temperature (Farenheit / Celcius)
Beef & Pork (Steaks Roasts Chops)	145F (62.8C)
Ground Meat	160F (71.1C)
Poultry	165F (73.9C)
Fish & Shellfish	145F (62.8C)
Ham (Precooked)	140F (60C)
Leftovers	165F (73.9C)

Pro Tip: How to Tell if Chicken is Cooked

When it's close to done, poke the chicken with a knife or fork. If the juices that run out are clear that means it's fully cooked. If the juices are pink the chicken needs more time.

GROCERY LIST

DATE:
_____

FRUITS AND VEGETABLES

DAIRY AND EGGS

MEAT AND SEAFOOD

FROZEN FOODS

PANTRY STAPLES

BREADS AND GRAINS

BEVERAGES

SNACKS AND SWEETS

HOUSEHOLD ITEMS

GROCERY LIST

DATE:
_____

FRUITS AND VEGETABLES

DAIRY AND EGGS

MEAT AND SEAFOOD

FROZEN FOODS

PANTRY STAPLES

BREADS AND GRAINS

BEVERAGES

SNACKS AND SWEETS

HOUSEHOLD ITEMS

WEEKLY MEAL PLAN

MONDAY

TUESDAY

WEDNESDAY

THURSDAY

FRIDAY

SATURDAY

SUNDAY

GROCERY LIST

WEEKLY MEAL PLAN

GROCERY LIST

MONDAY

TUESDAY

WEDNESDAY

THURSDAY

FRIDAY

SATURDAY

SUNDAY

Recipe

NAME OF DISH: ....

INGREDIENTS:

- ....
- ....
- ....
- ....
- ....
- ....

- ....
- ....
- ....
- ....
- ....

PREP TIME:

COOK TIME:

SERVES:

DIRECTIONS: ....

....

....

....

....

....

NOTES:

Recipe

DIFFICULTY:

☆ ☆ ☆ ☆ ☆

NAME OF DISH: ....

INGREDIENTS:

-
-
-
-
-
-

-
-
-
-
-
-

PREP TIME:

COOK TIME:

SERVES:

DIRECTIONS:

....

....

....

....

....

....

NOTES:

FITNESS FACTS

1 The CDC reports that regular exercise can reduce the risk of depression by up to 25%.

2 As we age the effect that exercise has on our body actually increases. This is why it's so important to get into good fitness habits now.

3 Engaging in at least 150 minutes of moderate-intensity aerobic exercise per week has been linked to a reduction in breast cancer risk in women by as much as 20-30%.

4 Physical inactivity is estimated to be responsible for approximately 6% of global deaths each year. In fact, according to the World Health Organization (WHO), physical inactivity is associated with a higher risk of death than smoking!

How to
BUILD A WORKOUT PLAN
That You'll Actually Use!

If improving your fitness is a serious goal for you, take time at the end of each week to write out a new plan for the coming week. If you just want to maintain a good regimen, you can make one daily or weekly plan and adjust it only when you need to.

Reserve time for at least one hard or challenging workout (like a long run or ride) per week, plus a mix of weightlifting, moderate-intensity cardio workouts, and rest days. Even if you only have time for shorter workouts of 10 to 20 minutes, that's still worth it. Don't let you brain trick you into thinking otherwise!

Use one of the planners on pages 107 & 109 to guide you

Exercise Generally Falls Into *2* Categories:

CARDIO

+

Exercise like cycling, running, and swimming, which get your heart pumping and blood flowing. This type of exercise builds aerobic fitness, endurance, and stamina.

STRENGTH TRAINING

Exercises that use weight to build muscle and strength, like lifting weights or bodyweight exercises like push-ups. These exercises foster strength and stability.

A combination of the two (alternating cardio and strength-building days, or incorporating both types of exercise into a day's routine) allows you to create an ideal workout plan.

How Much Should You Exercise?

Adults need at least 1.5 hours of moderate-intensity cardio activity (like a brisk walk), and two days of muscle-strengthening per week to maintain good physical and mental health. If you're already comfortable with regular exercise, you can aim for that 150 to include 75 minutes of high-intensity activity (like jogging or cycling).

Don't Rush Into It!

As a general rule, aim to work out three days per week as you ease into a new fitness routine. Such a schedule gives your body downtime to recover and adjust—which is just as important as your exercise sessions.

Cross-Training

Cross-training means mixing up the kinds of exercises you do instead of sticking to just one. It's like having a variety pack of workouts! So, instead of always running or only lifting weights, you could try a sport, swimming, cycling, yoga, or even dancing. By doing different activities, you work out different parts of your body and stay healthier overall. Plus, it keeps things fun and interesting!

Cross-training can also help prevent overuse injuries that can result from doing the same repetitive movements over and over.

As You Become Stronger...

As you progress with your training you can start to boost both the volume and intensity of your routine. Consider including exercise on days that were previously designated as rest days. You could also divide your strength training sessions into upper- and lower-body focused days. For instance, you can target arms and abs on Mondays and Wednesdays, and concentrate on glutes and calves on Tuesdays and Thursdays. This way, each muscle group has time to fully recover while you continue exercising daily.

How To Keep It Going

Don't start off too strong
People start a new routine with a lot of excitement and motivation which is great... until they push themselves TOO hard and get injured or burnt out right off the bat.

Always Use Proper Form
One push-up in proper form is worth 10 in bad form. Bad form is how you injure yourself and lose a lot of benefit from any exercise, so keep that back straight and head up!

Make It Fun
The easiest way to keep your motivation for fitness is to make it fun. Incorporate activities you love, and switch things up on a regular basis. For extra fun AND motivation, try working out with a friend or two.

Keep it Consistent
Even if you can't manage the whole routine, if you had a plan to work out then modify it. Any exercise is better than none.

When it comes to health, our needs vary from person to person, so please check with your doctor before making any big changes to your physical training or lifestyle.

Major Muscle Groups

Making sure all muscle groups are targeted in your weekly routine is key to a well-rounded workout plan.

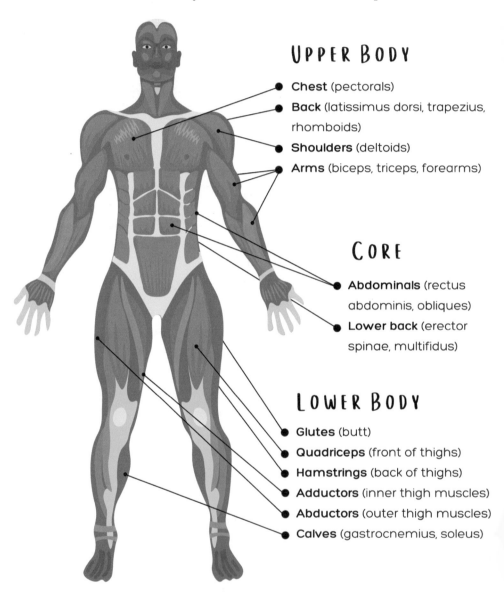

Upper Body

- **Chest** (pectorals)
- **Back** (latissimus dorsi, trapezius, rhomboids)
- **Shoulders** (deltoids)
- **Arms** (biceps, triceps, forearms)

Core

- **Abdominals** (rectus abdominis, obliques)
- **Lower back** (erector spinae, multifidus)

Lower Body

- **Glutes** (butt)
- **Quadriceps** (front of thighs)
- **Hamstrings** (back of thighs)
- **Adductors** (inner thigh muscles)
- **Abductors** (outer thigh muscles)
- **Calves** (gastrocnemius, soleus)

Did You Know...

Muscles Have Memory! Muscle memory is a real thing where muscles "remember" repeated movements or exercises, making it easier to perform those movements in the future. This is why any physical skill become easier with practice, as the muscles involved become more efficient at performing those tasks.

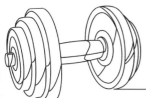# WORKOUT PLANNER

Exercise	Reps	Sets	Time

Cardio	Calories	Distance	Time

Notes:

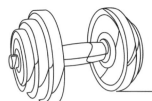

WORKOUT PLANNER

Exercise	Reps	Sets	Time

Cardio	Calories	Distance	Time

Notes:

WEEKLY WORKOUT PLANNER

Monday	R E P S	S E T S
Cardio:		

Tuesday	R E P S	S E T S
Cardio:		

Wednesday	R E P S	S E T S
Cardio:		

Thursday	R E P S	S E T S
Cardio:		

Friday	R E P S	S E T S
Cardio:		

Saturday	R E P S	S E T S
Cardio:		

Sunday	R E P S	S E T S
Cardio:		

"The difference between the impossible and the possible lies in a person's determination."

- Tommy Lasorda

WEEKLY
WORKOUT PLANNER

Monday	R E P S	S E T S
Cardio:		

Tuesday	R E P S	S E T S
Cardio:		

Wednesday	R E P S	S E T S
Cardio:		

Thursday	R E P S	S E T S
Cardio:		

Friday	R E P S	S E T S
Cardio:		

Saturday	R E P S	S E T S
Cardio:		

Sunday	R E P S	S E T S
Cardio:		

"The difference between the impossible and the possible lies in a person's determination."

- Tommy Lasorda

HOW TO GET YOUR FIRST *Lambo!*

...BUT MOSTLY OTHER CAR STUFF

Okay, okay, I'm not quite going to tell you how to get a lambo. But you're smart, you're reading this guidebook and using the tools - you're already on your way!
And if you really want it laid out...

Step 1. Plan
Step 2. Work hard at worthwhile things
(Step 2.5. Assess progress and keep planning)
3. Save and build your wealth
It really is that simple!

NOW ON TO OTHER CAR STUFF...

If you weren't lucky enough to grow up learning how to fix cars, or born with an innate sense of negotiation, buying and owning a car may seem a bit overwhelming.

Not to Fear!

The next few pages are all about buying a car, keeping it in good shape, and not breaking the bank doing it.

THINKING ABOUT AN EXPENSIVE CAR?

Set a goal!

BUT...

...for your own sake, be real about it.

A "luxury" car can range from 33k USD into the millions. The above-mentioned lambo? A bare bones model will cost you around 200k USD, the same price as some homes out there.

Yes you can finance a car, and do check out our section on financing (and section on Money). But adulting means thinking long-term.

If you need a car, consider how a smaller sacrifice now could mean a much greater benefit down the road.

Buying a Car

The Negotiation

Big ticket items like cars are one of the few places you can negotiate. Remember to do your research beforehand. Confidence is key! Whatever you do, stay firm in your own mind about the limits of your budget and never be afraid to say no and walk away. There's probably a dealership down the road that will give you a better price for the exact same car.

- Buy your car at the end of the month. Dealerships have quotas they have to meet so they'll be more motivated to cut you a good deal.

- You CAN negotiate the interest rate, don't let them tell you otherwise. The bank will give them one interest rate but they can easily go in and up the percentage in order to get more money from you.

- Finance guys want you to buy their used car warranty. Use this to your advantage if you were already planning on buying one - it's usually a good idea anyway. Tell them you'll buy the warranty IF they reduce the interest rate or price.

- You don't want to pay MSRP (Manufacturer's Suggested Retail Price). Ask for the invoice that shows what the dealership paid for the car. You want to pay as close to that as possible.

- If you are financing the car, they will try to get you to focus on the monthly payments. Instead, focus on the actual price of the vehicle and how to reduce the compounding interest you'll pay.

Trading in Your Old Car?

- Don't tell them you have a trade-in until you have your new car picked out with the price agreed upon. You'll end up getting a better deal.

- Don't tell them how much you want to trade in your car for. They might have had a higher price in mind, but you blew it when you gave them your price which was lower.

- When they walk around your trade-in they will quietly touch all the dents and dings. Keep quiet! This is a psychological trick to make you tell on yourself, so when they lowball you with the price, they can use what you said against you.

It's the best car in the world! (it's not)

Buying a Car
NEW OR USED

PROS

- Reliability
- Has a full warranty
- Has the newest features
- Low maintenance
- Usually has better fuel efficiency

CONS

- **Highest cost!!**
- Financing might be your only choice and lock you in for up to 8 years!
- Value depreciation- By the time it's paid off, what will the car be worth?
- Higher insurance cost

PROS

- Much lower cost
- Less depreciation
- Warranties are available
- Still possible to finance
- Still a new car for you!

CONS

- Higher maintenance cost
- May be less fuel efficient
- Warranty may be an extra cost, and may not cover everything
- There may have been past accidents which compromised the car (ask the salesperson, they have to tell you).

FINANCING
aka More Debt

You need to buy a car, but if you only have a few thousand dollars or less, you're not going to find anything to buy outright that won't need regular work. Spending thousands on a used car only to spend thousands more on constant repairs is a huge waste of money.

You can finance a car with a dealership but not if you're buying it privately. Financing means a loan through a bank, which the dealership arranges for you. You might want to buy privately, and that might be best for you if you have the cash. If you don't, financing a car through a dealership has advantages. Even though a dealership has higher prices, they're easier to hold accountable if the car turns out to be a lemon. In fact, financing a car can actually improve your credit as long as you are responsible with the payments. If you do decide to buy privately, take the car to a mechanic first, and make sure you get a vehicle history report online. These are well worth the cost, usually $15-$30.

Weigh Your Options:
When you're young and just starting to build your finances, the best thing is to have a car that's cost effective, reliable, low maintenance, and good on gas. Consider your circumstances and make the adult choice.

Taking Care of Your Car
← So This Doesn't Happen

Owning a car affords you a unique kind of freedom. You want to maintain that, so taking care of your car should be a priority. Car repairs also cost a lot of money, and investing in regular maintenance will mean you save a lot over the long run.

Most drivers don't know a lot about cars. Unfortunately some mechanics take advantage of this. There are a lot of ways to save money when you own a car, and having a trusted and reliable mechanic is one of them. If you don't, it's even more important to be familiar with your car and what kind of regular maintenance it needs -and what it doesn't! The best mechanics get business from word of mouth, so ask around rather than taking your car to the first place you find. If there's an issue with you car, tell the mechanic in advance that before any work is to be done you need to know what the diagnostic is, and what it would cost to fix it. If your car needs a repair but is still drivable, you can always take it to another mechanic for a second (free) opinion. Compare the costs you're given to what you see with a quick online search.

Oil Changes

Engine oil is the lifeblood of your car. It keeps the engine running smoothly by lubricating the parts, capturing dirt and particles, and preventing corrosion. Over the course of about 6 months or 10,000 km of driving the oil gets too gunked up to do its job. That's when you need an oil change.

Most newer cars were designed for synthetic motor oil, as opposed to the traditional motor oil derived from crude oil. Older cars using regular oil will need more regular oil changes.

Tires

Air Pressure

Air pressure in your tires is measured in PSI, and gradually decreases over time. This is especially true the older a tire gets. Keep an eye on how your tires look. Filling it too much can be a risk too. Some like to keep a tire pressure gauge handy, they're small and cheap. Check the door jamb or owners manual for the correct pressure for your car's tires. The pressure listed on the side of the tire itself is the very maximum that should not be exceeded.

Tire Treads

This is the pattern of grooves on the surface of the tire that helps the tire grip the road. Tires need replacing once the tread has been worn down to about 1.6 mm.

Seasonal Tires

Make sure you have the right tires, winter, summer, or all-season. They're made of different material and can degrade faster if not being used under the proper conditions.

THE TUNE UP
Cars Need Check-Ups Too!

Once a new car hits about 100,000 km (62,000 mi), and then every 30,000-100,000 km (18,000-62,000 mi) afterwards it will need a tune up. Keeping on top of this important maintenance task will keep your car in great shape and save you a ton of headaches and costly repairs. There are a few things your mechanic will check on and may replace during a tune up:

Spark Plugs - These things get your engine started and maintain ignition across all cylinders.

Air Filters - Engine and cabin filters. This is pretty easy to change yourself if you are up for watching a couple of online videos. Some vehicles have a fuel filter as well.

Fluids - From oil to brake fluid, transmission fluid, and power steering fluid, there is a lot of liquid that your car needs to run. Flushing these periodically keeps the lines and engine from getting blocked with gunk which can cause serious damage.

Belts & Hoses - It's important to replace belts and hoses when they get wear and tear. This avoids having them break while you're on the road, potentially causing more damage to your car.

Engine Diagnostic - Hooking your engine up to a special device will identify any underlying issues with your engine specifically.

 Always look out for this engine symbol on your dashboard. Take your car in as soon as you can if it comes on.

ALSO:

Roadside Assistance: This is a subscription service, like CAA or AAA that will come help you if your car breaks down, whether it's a battery boost you need or a tow. They'll come open your doors when you lock your keys in your car too!

You can do some things on your own!: Topping up fluids, changing filters and switching out tires are fairly easy tasks. Just watch a few online videos for your specific make and model of car and you can save some serious bucks.

THINGS TO KEEP IN YOUR CAR

- Fuzzy dice (of course)
- Something for trash (bag, box, whatever)
- Microfibre cloth (cars get dusty!)
- Multipurpose spray cleaner
- Car manual
- Insurance & Ownership Papers
- Paper & Pen

WINTER SAFETY

- Snow Brush & Ice Scraper
- Salt (melts ice and useful for grip)
- Candle (to create heat if you're stuck in the car)

EMERGENCY ITEMS

- Spare Tire & Tire Jack
- Extra Water & Snacks
- First Aid Kit
- Extra Wiper Fluid
- Thermal Blanket
- Paper Map
- Jumper Cables
- Cones
- Flashlight & Candle

EMERGENCIES

If you encounter an emergency situation while driving, do the following:

1. Put your hazard lights on.
2. Pull over safely.
3. If you need to, exit on the side of the car not facing traffic.
4. Put your hood up and place cones behind your car.
5. Call for help or flag someone down for assistance.

Pro Tip Keep things clean with a car vacuum. It's like a dust buster that plugs into your car charger. Just don't get caught vacuuming when the light turns green!

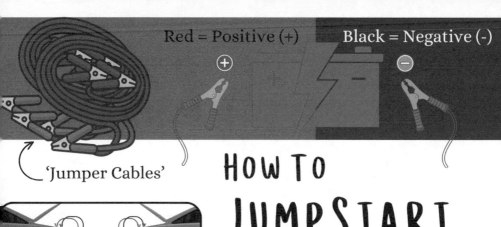

Red = Positive (+) Black = Negative (-)

'Jumper Cables'

HOW TO
JUMPSTART
A CAR

1 Position a car with a charged battery nose-to-nose (but not touching) with the vehicle with the dead battery. Here's where having long cables helps. Turn the ignition off.

2 Locate the positive (+) and negative (-) terminals on the car batteries. The (+) may have a red plastic cover or flap. Brush away any loose rust or battery acid.
In a minute you're going to clamp the cables onto the terminals, basically attaching to the whole or part of the round metal pieces sticking up.

3 Connect the 4 cables to the car batteries in this order:
1. Red cable --> live battery (+) terminal
2. Other red cable --> dead battery (+) terminal
3. Black cable --> live battery (-) terminal
4. Other black cable --> dead battery (-) terminal

If the car still won't start, it may be that your battery needs to be replaced, or the working battery is too small to jumpstart a larger vehicle.

4 Start the working car. Let it run for a minute before trying to start the dead car. You may need to pump the gas a bit to get it going. Once it starts, LEAVE IT RUNNING! The other car can turn off.

5 While the car is running, detach the cables in the opposite order you put them on.
Now you're good to go!

REMEMBER: ONCE YOUR CAR IS RUNNING AGAIN YOU MUST DRIVE YOUR CAR (NOT LET IT SIT RUNNING IN YOUR DRIVEWAY) FOR AT LEAST 30-40 MINUTES TO RECHARGE YOUR BATTERY. OTHERWISE IT MIGHT NOT START NEXT TIME.

RENTING

It's a Beautiful Thing,

A home of your own. Hello living room hot tub! (Or whatever crazy thing you have planned)

Reality Check

Finding a new place is definitely exciting - at first. Oh you'll find your perfect place... but most likely it'll be 5 times more than what you can afford. That's ok! That SHOULD be the goal for one day, but for now linoleum kitchen floors and appliances from the 80's will do just fine. The squeaky floorboards and your creative storage methods will be part of the hilarious memories you'll look back on fondly one day. Trust me - this is a rite of passage. So keep an open mind when apartment-hunting. The right place will find you, and you'll make it AMAZING!

Things to Consider:

Price

DO NOT spend more than half your income on rent. Ideally you'd spend about 33 percent. If you consider going outside your budget, just consider what you'd have to give up to make it work, and how stressful it would be always worrying about having enough money for the bare necessities.

Location

*Is it close to transportation? How about work? Is there a corner store you can walk to?
*Are there noisy things nearby? Airports? Busy parking lots with dumpsters? Frat houses? Dog kennels?
*How's the neighbourhood? What is the crime rate like? How comfortable would you feel walking alone there at night? Speaking of which, how's the security at the building?

What's Included

Hydro? Heat? Water? Cable? Some places include some or all of these, others don't. It makes a difference to your budget.

The Landlord / Owners

Bad landlords make your life horrible. If your gut tells you this one is no good, trust it.

HOW TO FIND A PLACE TO RENT

 Once you find a place you like, fill out an application form. This includes references, either past landlords or other authority-type figures in your life. It will also probably include a credit check. Yet another reason to keep your score high.

 If you're approved to move in, you sign the lease and make a deposit. The amount is different depending where you are. Sometimes it's first and last month's rent. Sometimes it's a security deposit you get back when you move out, or that they use to pay for unreasonable damage you caused.

 Move-in day is usually the first day of the month, but that can sometimes be negotiated. You'll arrange a time to meet the landlord or superintendent (the person who takes care of the building) there on that day. You'll get the key and do a walkthrough. That's it! Time to move in!

THE WALKTHROUGH

This is where you walk through the place with the landlord/super and look over what shape everything is in with a checklist they have. If your landlord doesn't automatically do this, BE SURE to insist on it. Make sure ANY damage is noted. This protects you so when you move out they don't charge you for damage that you didn't make.

TENANT INSURANCE
And What the Heck is a Deductible?!

You may or may not be required by your landlord to have tenant insurance. If you even have a few nice things, electronics for instance, it's probably worth it anyway. It's pretty cheap, and besides certain types of damage, it covers any personal items you have in your home that you list with the insurance company. When you purchase the insurance policy you will review everything you want to insure, and each item's value.

Oh...and deductibles... this is an amount you have to pay first before your insurance company pays for whatever the remaining cost is. The lower the deductible, the higher the insurance rate.

TENANT RIGHTS
Know What to Expect Before You Rent

Now that you're an adult, you need to know your rights, and be willing to stand up for them. I hate to say it, but not all landlords are wonderful. Some think young adults, or just adults in general, aren't going to know much about their rights and try to take advantage of that. Not this time though... not you! You're smart, you've done your research, and you know what's what.

Let's be honest, it's hard being a small fish in a big pond, like a young adult in a sea of weathered grownups. But come on, you're no newborn babe. You've been around the block, so don't underestimate yourself. You deserve and should demand the same treatment from your fellow adults as they would give any other, and of course you need to give the same in return. Find confidence in this and remember it when you are walking into situations where you're negotiating with or asking for something from a landlord or an authority figure.

YOU WANT TO BE A GOOD TENANT!

First because you're not a jerk, but also because if something goes wrong (your toilet broke, you have bedbugs, your neighbour blasts music all hours of the night and won't stop), you want your landlord to have your back. Even though they're supposed to anyway, they're going to help you a lot faster if you've built a good relationship with them. They'll go out of their way to keep you there, because they're invested in keeping good tenants. On the other end, landlords can make living there a real headache for tenants that do the same for them.

Residential Laws are made at the state, provincial, or territorial level. This means whatever territory, province or state you live in, that's where you can go to find out your specific tenant rights. See how they compare to your lease.

Find out the specifics in your area about the following:

Rent Control: Some places have regulations that limit how much and how often a landlord can increase rent.

Lease Agreements: The laws dictate the terms and conditions that can be included in a lease agreement, such as the length of the lease, the amount of rent, and the responsibilities of both parties. If you see something that seems unreasonable in the lease, check before you sign. You can always try to negotiate.

Security Deposits: Rules about the maximum allowable amount, conditions for withholding when you move out, and the timeframe for returning deposits, are usually outlined.

Maintenance & Repairs: The responsibilities of landlords and tenants regarding maintenance and repairs are usually specified. Landlords are generally required to ensure that the rental property meets health and safety standards. Be familiar with this, as some landlords will try to avoid necessary and health-related repairs to save money.

Evictions: The process and grounds for eviction, as well as the rights of tenants facing eviction.

Privacy: Laws often address the landlord's right of entry into the rental unit and specify under what circumstances they can enter without the tenant's permission.

IF YOU HAVE A MAJOR PROBLEM, THERE ARE PLACES THAT CAN HELP

- **Local Tenancy Board** (Canada) - they take complaints and have authority over local landlords.
- **Landlord Tenant Court** (USA) - ie. housing or small claims court, where tenants can file lawsuits against landlords.
- **Tenant Advocacy Organizations** - local or regional groups that have connections and can help advocate on your behalf.
- **Local Tenant Rights Hotlines** - only in some areas, but they can give advice about your specific issue and available options.

CONTRACT FROM THE BLACK LAGOON

Where Others Would Run...

THIS RENTAL
CONTRACT
IS NO MATCH FOR A
LEGENDARY ADULT

Quick, decipher these important contract
terms ... before it's too late!

1. TEILITUES

_ _ _ _ _ _ _ _ _

2. HITGR OT NREET

_ _ _ _ _ _ _ _ _ _ _ _

3. PTDOIES

_ _ _ _ _ _ _

4. SEPRRAI

_ _ _ _ _ _ _

5. EFER IIWF

_ _ _ _ _ _ _ _

6. NGTOIBEEAL

_ _ _ _ _ _ _ _ _ _

7. EVTCIONI

_ _ _ _ _ _ _ _

8. RVICYAP

_ _ _ _ _ _ _

9. TANMCEANIEN

_ _ _ _ _ _ _ _ _ _ _

10. BTSONRFIS

_ _ _ _ _ _ _ _ _

(This one should NOT be in there!)

ROOMMATE AGREEMENTS
This Will Help You

*L*iving on your own for the first time can be so much fun when you're doing it with a friend or two. Not only does it take some pressure off your finances, having someone else there to help figure out what to do when the internet goes down or the toilet is overflowing can be very helpful!

People have all kinds of lifestyles though. Don't find out the hard way that yours is incompatible with your roommate's. Your best buddy might be great, but if they love cooking meat for breakfast lunch and dinner while you're a vegetarian, that might be an issue.

Living together takes at least a little cooperation. Laying all the expectations out in a written agreement AHEAD of time will ensure you're both on the same page right from the start. Then, if anything goes wrong, you'll be protected. Moreover you'll have a reference point to refer to if there is ever any confusion about what was agreed upon.

Keep in Mind: If your roommate is consistently ignoring their agreed-to responsibilities, or refuses to acknowledge when they make a mistake (come on, we're all human!), then consider that roommate agreements can be ended and that it may be time to do so.

A FEW THINGS TO CONSIDER BEFORE MOVING IN:

- Do your schedules align enough that you wouldn't drive each other crazy?
- Do you have any issue with the people in their life? Their significant other? What about the frequency that other people would come over?
- Do you feel confidant all parties are willing to share the workload equally?
- Does this person need a place for around the same timeframe as you?
- Are there any red flags like a history of failing to meet serious obligations, or being regularly unemployed?

WRITING A ROOMMATE AGREEMENT

You can use the template included on the next page, or you could write your own that is exactly suited to your needs.

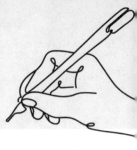

If you write your own, make sure you include the following:

1. Tenant names, and identifying if one is the primary tenant (ie. if only one person is on the actual lease).
2. The property address.
3. The date the lease begins.
4. The amount of rent each person pays, when, and how it's done.
5. Who pays for utilities.
6. Who pays the security deposit.
7. That all tenants share responsibility for keeping common areas clean.
8. Who buys food, or if you're each buying your own food.
9. That each person is responsible for damages they (or their pet, or guests) cause.
10. Signatures of occupants and the date signed.

You can end certain clauses with...

'...unless otherwise agreed to on a case by case basis',

so that everyone knows there can be the odd exception. The point is that it's agreed to beforehand and everyone's feelings are respected.

Optional things you may or may not want to include:

1. Rules around pets.
2. Rules for overnight guests (and how long a guest can stay).
3. What to do if you or they decide to move out.
4. A procedure to follow if there's a dispute.
5. The location of parking spaces and who pays for them.
6. Quiet hours.
7. Prohibition of drugs.
8. Under what conditions the roommate would be required to leave.

*if you don't know your new roommate well, definitely consider adding this last clause and including as much detail as possible. It's a contingency plan - hope you'll never need it but if you do you'll be so glad it's there.

Roommate Agreement

On _____, _____ , we, the tenants named below, signed a lease agreement for the residential property at the address listed below. By entering into this roommate agreement, we hope to ensure that rental responsibilities will be understood and shared by all roommates as described in this agreement.

Tenant #1 [print]: _____

Tenant #2 [print]: _____

Tenant #3 [print]: _____

This Roommate Agreement (the "Agreement") is made by and between the tenants listed above, for the residential property at:

[address]_____

This Agreement identifies the rights and responsibilities of each tenant during the course of the lease agreement.

This Agreement runs concurrently with the lease agreement for the residential property, which is effective from _____, to

_____,

1. SECURITY DEPOSIT: The total security deposit amount that we paid the landlord for the residence as required by the lease agreement is $_____, which was paid to _____ on _____. Individually, we each paid a portion of the security deposit as follows:

Tenant #1 _____ $_____

Tenant #2 _____ $_____

Tenant #3 _____ $_____

Each roommate will receive his/her share of the security deposit if and when the landlord returns it after the lease term ends. Any deduction(s) from the deposit by the landlord shall be withheld from all of the roommates in proportion to the amount of deposit that he/she paid. However, any damage to the residence caused by a particular roommate or roommates shall be charged only to the roommate(s) who caused the damage.

2. RENT: Under the terms of the lease agreement, the total rental amount due each month to the landlord is _____$. Each roommate shall pay the following amount:

Tenant #1 _____ $_____
Tenant #2 _____ $_____
Tenant #3 _____ $_____

Rent must be paid in the form of _____ to _____. The rent is due on the _____ day of each month.

3. HOUSEHOLD SUPPLIES: A single ledger (with item description, cost, and date of purchase) will be kept listing all household supplies purchased by each roommate. The supplies may include such things as paper towels, toilet paper, cleaning fluids, dish detergent, foil, plastic trash bags, scrub brushes, and any other goods needed for the home which will be shared by all roommates. The purchaser of household supplies will be entitled to partial reimbursement from the other roommates. Purchases will be agreed upon by all roommates before they are made.

4. KITCHEN USE AND CLEAN-UP: (check one)

____ Food expenses will be shared equally by all roommates.
____ Food will be purchased by each roommate individually.

Food may not be borrowed without the purchaser's approval. Each roommate will have storage space for their groceries. Roommates may choose to share in meal preparation and clean up. Each roommate will clean up the kitchen after his/her use.

5. CLEANING: Each roommate agrees to share the responsibilities of cleaning and maintaining common areas which may include dusting, vacuuming, emptying trash, mopping/sweeping floors, cleaning bathrooms, and other duties as agreed by all roommates.

6. UTILITIES
The following services have been arranged for as follows:

TYPE	COMPANY	ACCOUNT HOLDER	MONTHLY PAYMENT	HOW BILL IS SHARED	HOW BILL IS PAID
Electricity					
Water					
Internet					

This Agreement represents the complete and final understanding of the roommates' intent. Any modification to this Agreement must be in writing, signed by all roommates.

We, the undersigned, agree to the above terms.

ROOMMATE SIGNATURES:

Tenant #1 _____ date _____

Tenant #2 _____ date _____

Tenant #3 _____ date _____

Please note that this Agreement does not supersede the lease or any other agreement that tenants may have with the landlord. The landlord is not bound by this Agreement and is not obligated to enforce its terms.

JOHNNY IS NOT IMPRESSED.

Help Johnny's s roommate
unscramble his fair share of the chores

1. ENGISEWP

_ _ _ _ _ _ _ _

2. DYLUANR

_ _ _ _ _ _ _

4. HDSEIS

_ _ _ _ _ _

5. DTGUNSI

_ _ _ _ _ _ _

3. PMIGNOP

_ _ _ _ _ _ _

6. RTHOBOMA

_ _ _ _ _ _ _ _

7. OOSLRF

_ _ _ _ _ _

> What?

"Happiness is not the absence of problems, it's the ability to deal with them"

-Steve Maraboli

PERSONAL GROWTH

Here's a secret...

Almost every adult gets to a point when they realize they've got some mental baggage, and it's holding them back from the life they wanted to be living by now. It's a hard realization. Most repress the thought and distract themselves. An example of this is the fabled 'mid-life crisis', and it's about more than losing your looks and buying a sports car.

Youth doesn't last forever. It's the character you develop on the inside that carries you confidently into your later years...and trust me, they ARE coming. Have you gotten your first grey hair yet? This personal growth stuff is important!

This guidebook is a tool you can use for keeping your life in order, but it's also meant to show you that keeping your life in order is important so that you can focus on your personal growth and actually get to where you want to be! This last section will guide you in taking this next, most important, step. The challenge of staying true to yourself and finding your place in the world with confidence doesn't end when you turn 21, it's just beginning. Make the best use of your time so you can focus on building the person and life you want, *consciously*. That life is one where you feel comfortable in your own skin, confident in who you are, navigating the turbulence of adult life and thriving in it! Start this journey now so you don't have a rude awakening at 39.

There's a lot of hype around 'personal growth' these days. People are cashing in with meditation crystals and yoga socks, but don't get caught up in that - you don't need anything except your own beautiful self. Learn to be content simply being alone with yourself in silence. Reflect. Get to know yourself more, even those deep dark corners we usually keep hidden. They key is to stop distracting yourself from any uncomfortable feelings that come up. These feelings are usually linked to feeling inadequate in some way - no wonder we avoid them! Be curious about that, and everything else. You're human. Perfect in your unique imperfection. Be the adult who's okay with that reality!

In this Personal Growth section, you'll get advice on handling hard times, and learn how to train your brain to think and see the world in more productive ways. It will also give you a glimpse into how vast, how dynamic, how unbelievable our universe truly is. Not only that, you'll learn to reflect more on your inner universe - conscious and unconscious -which is just as vast and incredible, and a lot more powerful than you may have realized. You want to be an adult who knows how to mould this vehicle that is our mind-body, which we use to experience life. Adulthood is meant for exploration on a whole new level. Keep an open mind and maybe you'll find some new ideas in the next few pages that resonate. If something sparks for you then do some thinking, make a journal entry, do some research and see where it leads you.

STRESS
& What to Do With it

You already know that being an adult doesn't mean you have life all figured out. This may still feel like a shock, or maybe you've known for a long time that there are a lot of incompetent adults out there (a lot). Either way, it's a disappointing reality. But you may still believe that CEO or celebrity guru really has discovered the secret to a happy stress-free existence. Unfortunately, even the happiest most successful humans have a ton of stressful things going on. It's best to know this now. But many adults add stress to stress, trying to get unstressed so they can reach their goal but end up more stressed and further away from it.

The goal is not to eliminate stress, rather to use it.

Did You Know

Studies have suggested that plants have a positive impact on reducing stress. Reasons include cleaner air, connection to nature, aesthetics, and the mindfulness it takes to care for them.

A smart adult uses stress! Stress serves a FUNCTION in our lives... it's a little warning bell telling us to stop and reflect. What's causing us this stress? Is this a situation we can change? Is this something that will pass? Do we need to put more effort into something, or take better care of ourselves? Sometimes stress can simply be a reminder to reframe the situation. Instead of letting all your thoughts pile into your consciousness all at once, take control and consciously put your focus onto where it needs to be - on dealing with whatever is happening. Don't get caught up in the 'woe is me' trap. Instead, reflect. Is this even something you can control? If so, what can you do? If not, let it go. It is what it is, and this too shall pass.

Novice Adults

Too often we get caught up in stress, and it can get to the point where it becomes an addiction. Think about it. Complaining of unbearable stress has become a normal part of today's culture. This is not good! Pay attention and you'll hear adults bragging and competing over how overwhelmed their lives are with all the meaningless tasks they put on themselves and events they don't want to attend. What a waste! Be reflective, don't fall into this trap and your mind will be clear to focus on the important things.

Legendary Adult

• •

Stress IS real, and people today have a lot on their shoulders. Sometimes things happen you can't foresee, or maybe it's a bad situation you can't change. Plus you probably have a lot on your plate! However, you can choose to make changes. Make your mental health a priority and develop regular routines and strategies that will help best manage whatever stress you might have at any given time. Learn more about yourself, like what you struggle with, what triggers you, etc. Good mental health involves the ability to reflect, which will make taking action to solve any problem a lot easier. When you're feeling stressed, start by looking at the bigger picture. Adulthood is a roller coaster with great highs and great lows. The best part about being an adult is learning to appreciate and grow from both. And anyway, we all need the low points so we can truly appreciate the high ones.

• •

"The greatest weapon against stress is our ability to choose one thought over another."

-William James

CRITICAL THINKING
Forging New Mental Pathways

Psychology says: Neurons That Fire Together, Wire Together. This means the more you allow your brain to think the same thing or the same way, however wrong or biased it might be, the more hard-wired your brain becomes to always go down that same mental path. It becomes so natural our brain starts thinking it's the only path there is.

From an early age, all humans (including you and me) tend to develop biases that often lead us away from the truth. If we follow these biases over and over they become hard-wired neural pathways that limit our thinking and therefore our success throughout our lives. Think of it like ruts in a dirt road that a car's tires naturally want to follow.

Luckily, science is now realizing that our brains can create new neural pathways even in later life. This is called "Brain Plasticity", and it's great news for adults! It requires forcing your brain into a new thought pattern over and over; just like forcing the tires out of the old ruts until the new pattern becomes habitual - you create new ruts going in the direction you actually want! This takes conscious awareness of where you are now, as well as an idea of where you want to go. You just can't do it without honest reflection. As a future legendary adult, it's important to recognize your own subjectivity and bias, so you don't get hardwired into an old cynical grump who forgets about the joy and wonder that life can bring.

COGNITIVE BIAS

Cognitive biases are common patterns of irrational thinking. They can be unconscious or conscious, and we all have them. These biases can influence perceptions, decision-making, and problem-solving, leading us away from seeing what's really going on. Recognizing and understanding these biases is crucial for making more informed and objective decisions.

IMPLICIT BIAS
Unconscious attitudes or stereotypes that influence perceptions and decisions, often based on factors such as race, gender, or age.

CHECK OUT SOME DIFFERENT KINDS OF BIASES HERE AND ON THE NEXT TWO PAGES. DO SOME REFLECTION AND SEE IF SOME OF YOUR OWN PERSPECTIVES MIGHT BE LIMITING YOU IN SOME WAY.

Halo Effect

Generalizing a positive impression of a person to other aspects of their character, ignoring flaws or negative qualities.

Anchoring Bias

Relying too heavily on the first piece of information you get when making decisions, even if it's irrelevant.

Availability Bias

Relying on readily available information, often recent or vivid examples, rather than seeking a more balanced view.

Sunk Cost Fallacy

The tendency to continue investing in a decision or project based on past investments of time, money, or effort, even if the future costs outweigh the benefits.

Groupthink

The tendency of a group to conform to a common opinion, often resulting in poor decision-making due to a lack of critical thinking.

Confirmation Bias

Tendency to favour information that confirms one's beliefs while ignoring or dismissing information that contradicts them.

Dunning-Kruger Effect

A cognitive bias where someone with low ability at a task overestimates their ability, while those with high ability underestimate their own.

The next time you feel offended by someone, consider that one or more of these biases may be at play on their end. Understanding this can help us take things less personally, and avoid jumping to hasty conclusions.

Projection is when someone unconsciously puts their own unwanted feelings or thoughts onto another person. Instead of recognizing these feelings as their own, they see them in someone else. It's like blaming someone else for something you're actually doing or feeling.

For example, if you're jealous of a friend, you might accuse them of being jealous instead. It's a way for our minds to protect us from dealing with uncomfortable emotions by pretending they belong to someone else. This can happen without us realizing it and can affect how we see and interact with others.

RELATIONSHIPS

As humans, our connection to others is a prime factor in our quality of life. In terms of relationships, as a kid our family is naturally the priority. Eventually that shifts to friendships in adolescence and usually moves towards monogamous love partnerships as we get older. Relationships aren't all easy, and given they're so important to our lives it's a shame there isn't much formal education past kindergarten about how to relate to, understand, or behave with others.

Every person above the age of three has felt hurt by someone, and made other people feel hurt too. By the time some people reach adulthood they're so fed up and mistrustful that they believe it's better to avoid relationships altogether. Don't lose hope! The world is full of horrible AND wonderful people. Which kind are you keeping in your life? Always remember: we can consciously seek out and choose the people we welcome into our lives and give our time to. Sometimes saying goodbye to a destructive relationship is one of those hard decisions a real adult just has to make.

Here are a few other important things to remember when it comes to relationships:

Be Your Own #1 Relationship

You're the only one who will 100% always be there for you. Why would you treat yourself any worse than you'd treat someone else, let alone your closest friend?

Boundaries!

Make conscious decisions about what is important to you. Be okay with saying no. Don't be a doormat, speak your truth. I guarantee you'll get so much more respect for it, and from the right people, too.

Speak the Hard Truths

Conflict is the worst. Sometimes we think we're being kind by not being honest with someone, when in reality we are deceiving them in order to avoid an inevitable conflict. Being honest even when it's hard is the kindest thing we can do for someone we care about.

Romantic Relationships

- Be honest about what kind of relationship you want.
- In the beginning, talk about what's ok and not ok.
- Don't try to become what you think they want you to be - It's YOU they chose, not someone else!
- Prioritize and respect your person. Never talk behind them.
- Don't try to make them jealous - this destroys trust.
- Give them the benefit of the doubt.
- Don't string someone along if you know deep down it's a no. Just don't.
- **Be curious about who they are - A unique ocean of experience, knowledge, potential, and imagination... just like you!**

DRAMA:

There are actually a number of evolutionary and psychological reasons, as you will see below.

Another question is, why is drama typically associated more with younger adults than older ones? Drama can meet needs that less seasoned adults sometimes don't understand or know how to have met any other way. The problem is that drama causes us to waste a lot of energy on meaningless destructive things that bring nothing positive to our lives. Older adults have found better ways to get these needs met, and so can you!

Emotional Intensity: Drama often brings heightened emotions, which can be addictive. The rush of adrenaline and dopamine associated with that can make someone feel more alive and engaged, even if upset.

Novelty and Excitement: Drama can provide a break from the same-old. It also introduces novelty and excitement into relationships, even if negative.

Validation and Attention: Drama can be a way to seek validation and attention from their partner or peers. It can serve as a way to feel important and acknowledged.

Conflict Resolution: Since conflict is unpleasant, drama can sometimes be a backwards attempt to deal with an issue within the relationship. In this way the drama is a form of communicating without saying what's really going on.

Evolutionary Factors: Evolutionarily, drama in relationships might have served as a way to test the strength and commitment of partners. Dealing with drama together could have reinforced bonds and signaled dedication to the relationship. Lots of people "test" each other today in relationships. However, this is not a good way to build trust!

Social Influences: Cultural and societal norms, as well as media portrayals of relationships, can contribute to the desire for drama. People may internalize the idea that passionate, tumultuous relationships are more romantic or desirable. This idea also seems normal if that's how you grew up seeing caregivers acting.

Insecurity and Attachment: Insecure attachment styles or unresolved personal issues can lead people to create or exacerbate drama in relationships as a way to cope with their own insecurities or fears of abandonment.

SO WHEN YOU FALL INTO THE NEXT DRAMA SPIRAL...

A bit of mature reflection and humility will help you put things into perspective. Ask yourself if you really want this drama... it's up to you. Drama makes problems worse, not better. And remember - A Legendary Adult never gets involved in other people's drama!

Having a GROWTH MINDSET

"Believe those who are seeking the truth. Doubt those who find it."

-André Gide

Life would be so boring (and scary) if we could know everything. But why do so many adults pretend like they've got it all worked out? Have you ever met anyone who gets upset when you don't follow their advice? They do this because they are trying to put on a show to the world that they know all, and here you are telling them maybe they don't. They already know that, they just can't handle everyone else knowing it too. These are the people who believe happiness is achieved by being problem-free, and that a giant ego is a natural product of wisdom. (It's not!) Be wary of these adults.

The wisest adults know that ego is often just a protection mechanism for our feelings of inadequacy. These adults know a lot, but they know there's even more they don't know. What they HAVE learned however, is how to be curious. They know that everyone knows something they don't, and they respect their fellow humans for that. They also recognize we all have our own lenses we see the world through, and try to acknowledge how their own lens might be a little foggy at times.

Legendary Adults are always on the lookout for stories they and others might be telling which are keeping them from fully seeing what is true.

The wisest humans take joy in the amazing complicated crazy world we live in, and enjoy learning and growing from it throughout their lives. This is the growth mindset you should cultivate.

EGO

Ego refers to a person's sense of self and self-esteem. Our egos can lead us to have a distorted view of one's abilities and importance in relation to others. It can manifest as arrogance, defensiveness, or a constant need for validation.

Advice from the Legendaries

LEARN FROM MISTAKES!
(OTHERWISE WHAT WAS THE POINT?)

WHAT STORY ARE YOU TELLING YOURSELF?

Stories have helped us understand the meaning behind things since time immemorial. It's a good thing! Our brains can't possibly process every bit of information it receives, so in order to deal with that we filter some things and give greater meaning to others. This helps to explain why humans have developed some of the common biases we have. We create stories to organize information about the world and make it easier to remember and share. What meaning we give, as we know, will vary from person to person. That's why, in our goal of facing life's challenges head on, it's important to consider what stories we tell ourselves.

For example, many people today live with the story that humanity is doomed... no one is trustworthy, things are worse than ever, and everyone is out for themselves. That's a depressing story. On the other hand, telling yourself that everyone is basically good, that they all want to help deep down, and even evil corporations are run by nice human beings isn't a great story either because it can get you into trouble. Neither story is fully true or false. Reality is always a lot more nuanced. But whichever story you choose (and yes, it is a choice) will totally change your approach to the world around you, and yield very different results for your life.

We tell ourselves stories about everything - our past, our problems, our relationships, our potential, our future... and the stories might not even be the same from one day to the next. Have you ever believed something was true only to find out it wasn't? Of course you have... you're human and you tell stories! That won't change, but the stories themselves can, and the truest stories are the most examined ones.

HOW TO TELL A NEW STORY:
Reason by First Principles

To reason by first principles means to break down a problem or idea into its most basic truths or fundamental elements and then build up from there to form conclusions or solutions. This is a method often used in philosophy and other academic fields. By breaking down complex problems into smaller pieces and reasoning from foundational truths, we can gain a deeper understanding of any issue and even develop innovative solutions that weren't clear when we were relying solely on conventional wisdom or existing frameworks (ie. our stories).

If You Really Want to Understand Something, Search Everywhere!

HARD TIMES

Life is beautiful, but it's hard, and gets harder as you get older. This is the opposite to what we think when we're kids and can't wait to grow up. So what do adults do in the hardest times?

What should we do when we realize things are in fact worse than we ever imagined possible, horrible to a magnitude where you can't sleep, can't think, can't function? Maybe something bad happened or maybe nothing is even technically wrong. Either way, on the inside you feel this heavy black weight that you just can't shake, and maybe can't even explain. Plenty of expert-looking adults you pass by everyday are experiencing this this behind a competent smile.

There's no easy solution to hard times, especially if there really is something happening beyond our control. In many cases though there is a story we are telling ourselves about our current situation which may be limiting our ability to see a bigger picture. This is normal, there's no way to perceive the world except through our own lens. However our ability to shift our thinking, adjust that lens, even if forcefully and uncomfortably, and consider new possibilities - this is our superpower. It WILL mean the difference between simply suffering through challenges only for them to repeat or haunt us, and coming out the other end stronger for having learned something from it and clearer on how to minimize future anguish.

We can't control what the universe throws at us, we can only control how we respond to it.

REFLECT: Don't bury your head in the sand. We so often want to blame the wrong thing for a problem if the real source is just too uncomfortable or scary to face. But facing it and getting curious about it is the only way of getting rid of it, along with those negative feelings. Adults have to deal with harsh truths and make hard decisions, that's part of the job. Think about your problem as un-emotionally as you can, knowing you're strong, that this experience can make you stronger, and that this too shall pass.

LOOK AROUND:

Have the dishes piled up? Is there laundry all over the floor? Having clean organized surroundings will support an organized mind that can better understand and find solutions to your problem.

BE KIND TO YOURSELF:

You deserve it. Everyone does. How would you respond to a friend if they came to you with the problem you're facing now? The answer should be, the exact same way you're responding to yourself.

GET SUPPORT: Being vulnerable takes so much more courage than stuffing down our feelings. Find someone who you feel comfortable with. Tell them in advance if you just want to them to listen or if you want help finding a solution. We are not meant to be islands. If people in your life aren't there for you, find new ones! The world is full of amazing people. And hey, counselling is awesome!!

GRIEF

We grieve more than just loved ones throughout our lives. That mid-life crisis thing for instance is actually grief. As we age, phases of our lives end. Sometimes it's hard to realize that we can never return to our past selves, experience those same excitements, or have the same freedoms and abilities we once did. We can also grieve experiences that we know we will never have. As we age, certain opportunities are simply no longer there. The way to handle this kind of grief is no different from how we handle any kind. We move through the stages of grief at our own pace, hopefully ending with acceptance. This always involves facing our feelings rather than avoiding them. Acceptance does not mean something won't always be painful. A tragedy will always be painful. But other lenses, other realities can be in focus, such as how someone lived as opposed to how they died. Things like mindfulness and gratitude practice can help. How we respond to the very worst experiences we survive throughout our lives will largely determine our own level of inner peace, and ability to look positively into the future.

HOW TO
Defeat Your Fears

Fear holds us back in life. You already know that. I'm not talking about functional fears, like of dark alleyways and jumping between rooftops. (It's good if you're afraid of that!) Nor do I mean a fear of spiders or heights, unless its preventing you from living the life you want. I'm talking about the big fears... fear of failure, fear of rejection, fear of conflict, fear of (fill in the blank). These ARE preventing you from living the life you want.

The thing is, our society is hell bent on making us comfortable, and teaches us to avoid struggle at all cost. Society says if we must struggle now it's only so that we don't have to struggle in the future. Moreover, we are bombarded with distractions that push us to escape our fears and our personal struggles. Companies bank on us doing (and buying) everything we can so as NOT to deal with our issues. This isn't good!

Ancient cultures and even traditional cultures today around the world have Rites of Passage. Young people endure a difficult physical and mental challenge to prove themselves in order to officially become an adult. It shows the importance of struggle for the sake of itself. The youths endure the struggle and become stronger for it. Afterwards they understand the weight and responsibility of adulthood and of life in general. They have more appreciation for their elders and what they in turn have gone through. Most importantly, they learn how to find their own strength in the face of adversity. The next thing they face doesn't seem so scary.

You've heard it before: Face Your Fears. Easier said than done. It feels like a catch phrase. Facing your fear of spiders... okay. But what about a fear that you're not good enough? Or a fear that you're going to fail at life? These fears are hard enough to acknowledge let alone figure out how to deal with. But facing it is exactly what you need to do - turn towards it instead of away, as much as you can. Facing it doesn't mean struggling against it. It means saying "okay" and letting it be what it is. This really is the hardest part. You see, this is where we learn the most from life. We don't grow unless it's hard, and it's hard not to struggle against things we are terrified of. Luckily, once you start facing the truth - your perceived truth - it gets easier. You start to realize that your truth may not actually be the REAL truth. Then you get to work to find out what that really is.

Remember - you are not this fear! It's just a thought in your mind, along with the thought that sunsets are beautiful, and that herbal tea is gross. Put that fear in a bubble for a moment and just take a look. Maybe you could learn to like herbal tea. It's possible isn't it?

Confront The Fear

Do the thing or activity that you're afraid of

THE HOW:
1. Break it down. Every action is made up of many tiny ones. Considering each tiny action independent of the others makes things seem less overwhelming.
2. Take ONE tiny action. One small step further towards the goal is farther than you've ever gotten, and something to celebrate.
3. Don't go crazy. You don't need to go way outside your comfort zone right off the bat, that will only set you back. Do the same step, one tiny action, over and over until it's no big deal anymore. THEN try the next step.
4. Recognize that this is hard! Most people are too afraid to push themselves beyond what they think they can do (key word, think!). You're stronger and braver than that. Know that you will reach your goal. Imagine and actually try to feel the feeling you'll have when you achieve it. Do this often, patiently, and you'll start to become that person who feels those feelings naturally.

Confront the Feeling

The ultimate goal here is full acceptance, but it takes time. It starts with simply turning towards rather than away. It's truly a mental exercise that can transform your consciousness over time.

THE HOW:
1. Do you really want to get rid of this fear? Then make the decision to spend a few minutes at least once everyday to do this. When it's time, make sure you are in a quiet place alone.
2. Think about this fear, but rather than engage with it on an emotional level the way you normally do, just let it be there. It won't feel comfortable, but just sit with it. The fear is there. Imagine the fear as a physical thing. It's not you, it's separate. After all, we are not our feelings. Whatever you do, for this time, don't push the feeling away, just separate it from yourself. Observe.
3. Accept that what you're afraid of might be real. The worst COULD be true. Maybe you WILL fail over and over. Maybe you AREN'T good enough. Maybe they WILL leave you when you show them who you really are. Don't fight this. This is the thing we are constantly struggling against, conscious and unconscious. Again, just sit with it. Follow the thoughts all the way through for once... where does this all come from, and what would it it actually lead to? Be as real with yourself as you can.
4. Just as you accept the worst is possible, accept that the opposite is also possible. Sit with that now. Whatever the outcome, the world would continue turning. Joy would still exist, as would hate, love, birth, and death. What else wouldn't change if the fear was true, or came true? Again, separate yourself from the fear. It is there. You are here.
5. Do this regularly and over time your consciousness will shift. It will become used being immersed in the thing your mind is always pushing away, and realize that life actually continues. The fear will start seeming less and less relevant. For now you deserve patience and kindness, so give that to yourself.

WHEEL OF LIFE

The Wheel of Life is a great tool to help you identify how you could bring better balance into your life.
Think about the 8 categories below, and rate them in your life from 1-10.

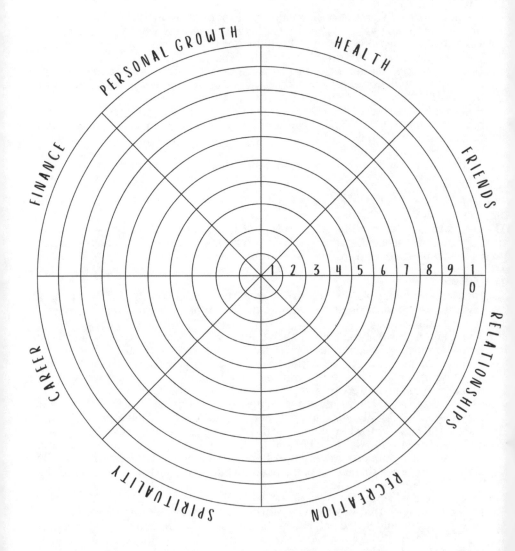

Did You Know HAVING A HEALTHY BALANCE BETWEEN THE AREAS OF YOUR LIFE MEANS YOU ARE MORE LIKELY TO EXPERIENCE IMPROVED EMOTIONAL RESILIENCE, INCREASED PRODUCTIVITY, AND ENHANCED SATISFACTION IN YOUR LIFE OVERALL.

"NO PROBLEM CAN BE
SOLVED FROM THE SAME
LEVEL OF CONSCIOUSNESS
THAT CREATED IT"

-Albert Einstein

THE *Shadow*

The idea of the Shadow is a big one in Psychology. It's another example of looking inward and dealing with the difficult realities you discover, in an effort to find acceptance and wholeness in oneself.

Most of us want to be good people, but we're also human so we fail at that sometimes. Are you able to admit that you've been selfish, mean, even cruel at moments in your life? You've also been jealous, hateful, manipulative, and maybe you possess an aggressiveness or a tendency to lie that is hard to control. These are very common traits, but not things that typically make you respect or want to be around a person, and for good reason. So what do you do when you find these traits in yourself? These are painful thoughts to have, and ones that are much easier to suppress, ignore, or deny (especially to ourselves).

Modern humans are pessimists with tunnel-vision. If we (or others) identify negative traits in ourselves - which is inevitable because we're not perfect - we can start believing that to be the basis of our identity. Naturally if 'who we are' is bad, anyone might feel the need to pretend to be someone they're not. This can all happen subconsciously without us even realizing it. All we know is, deep down we don't feel good about who we are and we put on masks to hide it.

The concept of the "Shadow Self" originates from the work of Swiss psychiatrist Carl Jung (pronounced "Yoong"), who proposed that each person possesses a hidden or unconscious aspect of their personality known as "the Shadow".

Those destructive personality traits you have are not your identity. They make up what is called the "Shadow Self" (termed by Carl Jung), and you can be certain everyone has one. But don't worry, the positive traits you possess are just as certain!

The problem is not the negative traits themselves, they're universal and inescapable. Think of them as POTENTIALS that we all possess. The problem comes when we allow them to manifest in our life in negative ways. Acknowledging them is step one to controlling them instead of the other way around.

INTEGRATING THE *Shadow Self*

Integration, for Jung, meant acknowledging and accepting these hidden aspects of ourselves rather than suppressing or denying them. By confronting and integrating the shadow, people develop a more authentic sense of self. Integration does not mean embracing bad tendencies or impulses. It means acknowledging these aspects without judgment and learning to channel them in healthy ways.

We Can't Escape Our Shadows... So Don't Try!

Take aggression for example. This is a trait that many people express in horribly unproductive ways today, but historically we needed violence to hunt and protect our tribes! So what are you going to do with your aggressive tendencies? You could be the person who will lash out or knock a guy out to save face. Or you could be the person who chooses to control their strength in the face of idiots, even though you could knock them out, and use it only when something is actually threatening the tribe. Which type of person is actually stronger?

Integrating your shadow self means accepting that you contain seemingly contradictory capacities and facets to your personality. Like the concept of Yin and Yang, both opposites are needed to be whole. Wouldn't you rather be whole than pretend to be some virtuous angel with no capacity for evil? You can never actually be that; we all have the capacity for evil. CONTROL those capacities, and that's an integrated shadow. KNOW you could do evil and choose not to, that's legendary adulting!

INTEGRATION AS HEALING

In more modern psychological approaches, such as trauma-informed therapy, the concept of integration plays a significant role in healing from past traumas and difficult experiences. Instead of merely seeking to eliminate traumatic memories or emotions, therapists work with clients to integrate these experiences into their overall sense of self. This process involves acknowledging the impact of trauma while also recognizing one's resilience and strengths. By integrating traumatic experiences into their own story and identity, people become empowered which leads to healing and growth. Integration-based approaches focus on honouring all parts of oneself, including those that may be painful or uncomfortable, as integral to one's whole self.

CELEBRATE WHO YOU ARE TODAY AND THE ENTIRE JOURNEY THAT HAS BROUGHT YOU HERE

How Are You Feeling?

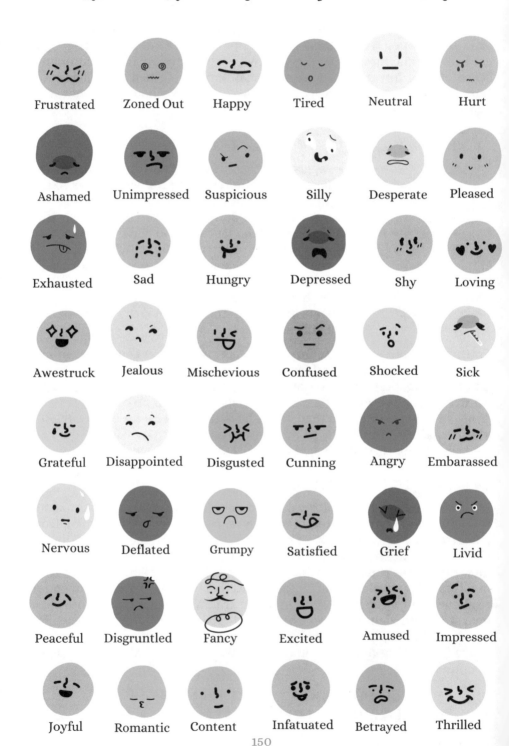

Frustrated	Zoned Out	Happy	Tired	Neutral	Hurt
Ashamed	Unimpressed	Suspicious	Silly	Desperate	Pleased
Exhausted	Sad	Hungry	Depressed	Shy	Loving
Awestruck	Jealous	Mischevious	Confused	Shocked	Sick
Grateful	Disappointed	Disgusted	Cunning	Angry	Embarassed
Nervous	Deflated	Grumpy	Satisfied	Grief	Livid
Peaceful	Disgruntled	Fancy	Excited	Amused	Impressed
Joyful	Romantic	Content	Infatuated	Betrayed	Thrilled

2-WEEK
MOOD TRACKER

1 2 3 4 5

DATE	MOOD(1-5)	INFLUENCES
/ /		
/ /		
/ /		
/ /		
/ /		
/ /		
/ /		
/ /		
/ /		
/ /		
/ /		
/ /		

POST-REFLECTION

"The happiness of your life depends upon the quality of your thoughts."
- Marcus Aurelius

2-WEEK
MOOD TRACKER

☹ ☹ 😐 🙂 😊
1   2   3   4   5

DATE	MOOD(1-5)	INFLUENCES
/ /		
/ /		
/ /		
/ /		
/ /		
/ /		
/ /		
/ /		
/ /		
/ /		
/ /		
/ /		

POST-REFLECTION

"The happiness of your life depends upon the quality of your thoughts."
- Marcus Aurelius

MINDFULNESS

Mindfulness is a mental state of focused awareness
and non-emotional acceptance of one's thoughts, feelings, and sensations in the present moment. It involves intentionally paying attention to what's actually going on right now without getting caught up in thoughts about anything else. Part of the idea is understanding that our minds have a hard time maintaining focus. Mindfulness teaches us to notice when the mind wanders, then to bring it back to the focused state, no frustration involved. Just notice, and bring it back. Soon your mind will wander less. Getting your brain used to thinking this way will help you notice what's going on around you and within you, which in turn means a lot less mental turmoil and confusion. Meditation and mindful awareness are the keys to shifting your consciousness, thus transforming yourself and your own reality.

MINDFUL MEDITATION

Mindful Meditation is one way that you can build up your brain's mindful muscle.

TO START: Sit or lie down somewhere quiet (ish), with no distractions.

THEN,

1. Focus your attention on your breathing. Breathe in for four slow breaths. Breathe out for four slow breaths. Repeat.

2. Inevitably your mind wanders. No big deal. Just notice this.

3. Gently bring your focus back to your breath.

HOW TO QUICKLY FALL ASLEEP AT NIGHT

- ☀ Avoid naps in the daytime

- 🛏 Make your bedroom comfy

- 🪷 Try some aromatherapy

- 🎵 Listen to relaxing music or sounds

- 📵 Switch off the screen 30 minutes before bed

GRATITUDE
Say Thank You for What You Have

♥

AND FOR WHAT YOU DON'T YET HAVE

Whether or not you believe in a higher power to thank, regularly experiencing the emotions associated with gratitude can have a huge impact on your life. In fact, modern science is just now starting to catch up with this concept. It's a theme that runs like a thread through all ancient spiritual beliefs, teaching us that when we align the energy we give off with the energy of what we love and want, this actually has an effect on the quantum field around us (the ancients used different terms to describe this) - and science today tells us that this quantum field is the fabric of our reality.

Today in our society, like many things with underlying truth, the concept of Gratitude has been glossed over and watered down by corporate schemes to sell it to you in the form of gratitude journals, inspirational posters, and motivational speeches about attracting abundance. Forget all that.

THE SCIENCE OF GRATITUDE...

Quantum Mechanics studies the very tiniest bits of matter and space. On that minuscule scale (one which our feeble human brains can't truly comprehend), the laws of classical physics don't make sense anymore. On that scale, according to quantum field theory, all particles and forces are understood as vibrations in underlying fields. These fields pervade all of spacetime, and their interactions give rise to all the phenomena we observe in the universe.

(Before I go on, you should know that this is an EXTREMELY limited way to describe an EXTREMELY complicated topic which is already a bit controversial, and which science is just starting to understand. Consider this a disclaimer and do your own research. You won't regret it!)

In essence this means that all matter including our body actually IS vibrational energy, oscillating at varying rates, ie. frequencies. Moreover, we now know that the tiniest bits of matter (particles like electrons, neutrons, and quarks) exist not only as tiny solid objects but also as waves, until observed. Let that sink in. This means all matter exists as potential up to the point that conscious awareness is focused on it, at which point it collapses into a fixed form. This means all potential realities, universes, exist on a quantum level. This is where the Multiverse Theory comes in. Not only that, all particles of matter-energy are connected by various quantum phenomena and systems, like a universal net. The behaviour of particles on one side of the net has an effect on those on the other side. So what does this have to do with gratitude? Bear with me...

We know that vibrational frequencies and potential energy are fundamentally what matter is; its physical form depends on consciousness, and frequencies affect the vibrations and behaviour of other particles - ie. physical reality - even when separated by great distances. The next question is, to what extent can one manipulate the frequency of matter? What happens when frequencies are tuned and synced? To what degree can our consciousness affect our reality on a quantum level?

Maybe humans have been doing it all along, just not in the lab, and maybe without even knowing it!

The Power of Sound

Did you ever wonder why sound was such an important part of ancient spiritual practice all around the world? There was a belief that certain musical tones (think frequencies) allowed a person to access a higher consciousness and become closer to the Higher Power. It also played roles in healing rituals. It was about syncing one's frequency with that of some higher plane of existence. Did ancient adults know something we don't?

The field of Cymatics today studies the vibrational effects of sound frequencies. There are many amazing online videos where you can see intricate geometric patterns and structures emerge in various materials such as liquids, powders, and solids when exposed to the vibrational effects of sound frequencies.

A Thought Experiment: What if those modern miracles we see from time to time - the terminal cancer patient who believes they'll survive and actually does, or when you randomly think about a long lost friend before bumping into them 10 minutes later, or the mother who lifts a truck off her baby even though it's physically impossible, or even the placebo effect - what if these are examples of frequencies aligning and quantum fields being manipulated in ways we simply don't understand yet? Just imagine what would be possible if we did!

Here's Where It Gets Crazy...

Everything emits vibrational energy, including us. Studies have shown over and over that our emotions actually determine the frequency of energy that we emit. Energy fields emitting from one group of study participants practicing gratitude were measured up to 3 meters from the subjects. The frequency we emit in turn affects what happens around us, potentially (if Quantum Mechanics is right) in a PHYSICAL way. A famous experiment called the Double Slit Experiment (seriously, look it up) shows us that on a quantum level, particles actually behave differently when someone is simply looking at them. This gives a lot of weight to the idea that simply putting our focus on something can change the outcome, and the emotion part seems to be the key.

Another study was done which purported to show that speaking and projecting negative or positive affirmations and emotions towards a glass of water affected the shape of the water crystals. Positive affirmations would create beautiful symmetrical patterns, whereas negative affirmations would cause the crystals to become fragmented and distorted. Interesting stuff, especially since human bodies are mostly water!

This link between vibrational frequency and emotion is clearly important. This is what gratitude practice is about at it's very core. The universe will reflect the energy you put out there. Instead of wishing for something to be different, practice the emotion you would have if it was already the way you want it to be. There's actual scientific evidence, not to mention ancient wisdom to support this. To sum it up, be grateful for what you have AND for what you don't yet have.

You don't have to take Science's word for it...

"Therefore I tell you, whatever you ask for in prayer, believe that you have received it, and it will be yours."
-Jesus (Mark 11:24)

30 DAYS OF GRATITUDE

Each day write down something, past or future, that you spent time appreciating.

DAY 1		DAY 16	
DAY 2		DAY 17	
DAY 3		DAY 18	
DAY 4		DAY 19	
DAY 5		DAY 20	
DAY 6		DAY 21	
DAY 7		DAY 22	
DAY 8		DAY 23	
DAY 9		DAY 24	
DAY 10		DAY 25	
DAY 11		DAY 26	
DAY 12		DAY 27	
DAY 13		DAY 28	
DAY 14		DAY 29	
DAY 15		DAY 30	

30 DAYS OF GRATITUDE

Each day write down something, past or future, that you spent time appreciating.

Day 1		Day 16	
Day 2		Day 17	
Day 3		Day 18	
Day 4		Day 19	
Day 5		Day 20	
Day 6		Day 21	
Day 7		Day 22	
Day 8		Day 23	
Day 9		Day 24	
Day 10		Day 25	
Day 11		Day 26	
Day 12		Day 27	
Day 13		Day 28	
Day 14		Day 29	
Day 15		Day 30	

SELF-CARE CHALLENGE

Increase Your Daily Water Intake	Take A Relaxing Bath	Set Goals For The Next Month
Learn A New Skill	Find A New Podcast To Listen to	Do A 10 Minute Guided Meditation
Disconnect From Social Media For One Day	Celebrate A Small Win From The Day	Get 8 Hours Of Sleep
Write Out A Bucket List	Do 30 Minutes Of Yoga	Read A Book

DID YOU KNOW

Laughing is good for the heart and can increase blood flow by 20 percent!

POP QUIZ

Q; How is Adulting like Whack A Mole?

a) Your kids wake you up with a mallet to the head

b) Moles eat all your home grown vegetables

c) Problems are like moles... as soon as you whack one down another one pops back up

d) All of the above

SOME FINAL WORDS

TO A CHILD, ADULTHOOD SEEMS LIKE A DESTINATION. NOW THAT YOU'RE THERE, YOU SEE THAT IT'S JUST ANOTHER BEGINNING - THE MOST EXCITING ONE YET!

Adulthood holds so much in store for you that you simply can't imagine yet. You'll have moments when the world will seem so beautiful and perfect you'll cry. You'll feel love one day that you never even knew was possible! One day you'll find yourself up against a brick wall with no where else to go but through - and somehow you will find a way to get to the other side of that wall! You'll do something that you didn't think you could, something REALLY hard, and whole new dimensions of the world around you will reveal themselves for the first time. It's truly incredible!

There are other moments on their way too, sucker-punches to the gut that are going to make you feel so much lower than you've ever felt in your life. Moments when some consequence of a choice you've made suddenly hits you and you realize that stupid choice can never be undone, and your life is pushed violently in a new direction because of it. It might feel like you can't possibly keep going. But you will.

Things are about to get REAL, and there's another moment in the future, rushing towards you at this very second, when you'll realize in a whole new way that your time here is limited. It's gonna feel scary. So what are you going to do with that?

Open the window, look around. It's beautiful out there. So take a deep breath, then take the next step forward.

You've got this!

SUMMING UP

So after all that, what IS adulting really about?
Well, it's a whole lot more than cooking, cleaning,
and making money...

MAKE A PLAN

You're all set when it comes to the planners, schedules and trackers. You know that getting organized is the key to getting the boring grown-up stuff out of the way. Now that the kitchen is clean and the bills are paid, you can focus on what's important - working on your real plan: becoming the best version of yourself, who has the confidence and mindset to create the life you always wanted. You can't do that if everything around you is chaos.

REFLECT, HONESTLY
(What Courage Really Means)

Don't lie to yourself. Face your sh*t. Look inward even when that's scary, and don't let your emotions control you. Being an adult means doing the hard thing, speaking the hard truths, and accepting the hard realities because deep down you know it's right. Things are the way they are, and only by seeing them this way, as a starting point, can we begin to move forward to change anything. Admit to your flaws and your mistakes - we all have them! We all make them! Only the bravest takes a true account of them, and that's mandatory in becoming a legendary adult.

WE CAN'T GROW UNLESS IT'S HARD

We can't learn anything when things are easy - period. The challenges we have to deal with and overcome give the most meaning to our lives because we grow from them. It's a doozy of a reality, but there it is.

THE PEOPLE IN YOUR LIFE

Make these choices consciously. Look around you. How are the people in your life dealing with this adulting stuff? It's not to judge, it's to realize that everyone - even the most competent people - has to face the challenges of being an adult. And people do it differently, don't they! The point is that you're no different. You could take one path or you could take another. The people around you will affect your choices. Our connections with other people become more and more important as we age, so choose ones that make it easier to become the person you want to be, not harder.

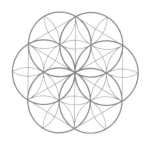

One Last Thing...
EVERYTHING IS CONNECTED

My God, the universe is complicated, and the older you get the more you realize how everything is connected in the most unimaginable ways. You'll see. We are beautiful complex beings, microcosms of the dazzling and terrifying whole that is our universe past, present, and future. We are each a tiny particle of that ONE, and the universe wouldn't be right if any piece of that was missing. Even the smallest happenings affect each other, and those connections are vast and unimaginable to us. With this in mind, one could say that everything happens for a reason. The Universe, the Higher Power, knows better than we do, so go with the flow. Accept everything that happens as an opportunity to grow. Speaking as one adult to another, I want to tell you that life is so worth living, so worth exploring, so worth being excited about!

Your story is just beginning, and it's up to you where you take it. You now know how limited we can be in how we see the world around us, but you also have some new knowledge you can use to see it more clearly. You now have greater insight into what a gift our mind-body truly is, and how you can shape it into exactly what you need to best navigate and influence this incredible reality you find yourself in. This is where your true power lies, because with this knowledge you can really and truly create the life you've always dreamed of. And with that my friend, you are officially on the path to Legendary Adulthood!

Remember, you have everything that this incredible
universe has to offer right at your fingertips.
It's up to you to go and get it!

"The more I learn,
the more I realize
how much I don't know."

-Albert Einstein

PASSWORD TRACKER

Website / Apps

Username

Password

Website / Apps

Username

Password

Website / Apps

Username

Password

Website / Apps

Username

Password

Website / Apps

Username

Password

Website / Apps

Username

Password

Website / Apps

Username

Password

Website / Apps

Username

Password

Website / Apps

Username

Password

Website / Apps

Username

Password

Pro Tip:
Don't use the same passwords for each site, that's how you get hacked

PASSWORD TRACKER

Website / Apps	Website / Apps
Username	Username
Password	Password

Website / Apps	Website / Apps
Username	Username
Password	Password

Website / Apps	Website / Apps
Username	Username
Password	Password

Website / Apps	Website / Apps
Username	Username
Password	Password

Website / Apps	Website / Apps
Username	Username
Password	Password

PASSWORD TRACKER

Website / Apps

Username

Password

Website / Apps

Username

Password

Website / Apps

Username

Password

Website / Apps

Username

Password

Website / Apps

Username

Password

Website / Apps

Username

Password

Website / Apps

Username

Password

Website / Apps

Username

Password

Website / Apps

Username

Password

Website / Apps

Username

Password

PASSWORD TRACKER

Website / Apps	Website / Apps
Username	Username
Password	Password

Website / Apps	Website / Apps
Username	Username
Password	Password

Website / Apps	Website / Apps
Username	Username
Password	Password

Website / Apps	Website / Apps
Username	Username
Password	Password

Website / Apps	Website / Apps
Username	Username
Password	Password

NOTES

Date: /   /

NOTES

Date: /   /

NOTES

Date: /   /

NOTES

Date: /   /

NOTES

Date: /   /

NOTES

Date: __ / __ / __

NOTES

Date: / /

NOTES

Date: /   /

NOTES

Date: /   /

NOTES

Made in the USA
Columbia, SC
18 December 2024

50053106R00098